NORTH DERBYSHIRE
TRAMWAYS
Chesterfield, Matlock & Glossop

This excellent study from 1913 shows the James Thompson (a local baker pictured on the tram platform) refreshment bandwagon on its way to Somersall, at the other terminus of the Chesterfield line, where he was contracted to supply the needs of some 2,000 children at their annual picnic. He hired one of the Brush 1904 cars for the occasion, seen here towing a water boiler running on an old horse car truck. This view, taken at the Whittington Moor terminus, shows a service car waiting in the distance. Vans such as Thompson's Belsize model seen on the left, had to take great care that their narrow-tyred wheels did not end up trapped in the grooves of the tram track.

NORTH DERBYSHIRE TRAMWAYS

CHESTERFIELD, MATLOCK & GLOSSOP

Barry M. Marsden

TEMPUS

A fine shot of one of the 1893 Milnes cable cars at the Crown Square terminus at Matlock, awaiting passengers for the steep one-in-five ascent up the bank to the right. The ornate tram shelter built in 1899 can be seen to the left of the tram, though it has not as yet received its elegant turreted clock, which is visible in later photographs. The shelter still survives in a nearby park, though the lettered glass panels are now preserved at Crich Tramway Museum a few miles away.

First published 2002
Copyright © Barry M. Marsden, 2002

Tempus Publishing Limited
The Mill, Brimscombe Port,
Stroud, Gloucestershire, GL5 2QG
www.tempus-publishing.com

ISBN 0 7524 2398 3

TYPESETTING AND ORIGINATION BY
Tempus Publishing Limited
PRINTED IN GREAT BRITAIN BY
Midway Colour Print, Wiltshire

Contents

Acknowledgements

In presenting this book I have many institutions and individuals to thank. As far as Chesterfield is concerned the mainstays have been the town's Local Studies Library, Chesterfield Borough Council, the former Chesterfield Transport Department, and Alan Bower with his monumental collection of old Chesterfield postcards. Between them they have generously provided vital material in almost equal measure. Other valuable contributions have emerged via Roger Kaye, the Tramway Museum Society (TMS) at Crich, Bob Young, whose mother was a tram conductress in the First World War, and David Beardsell. Others whose donations deserve mention include the late Len Rhodes, Transpire, J. Garrod, A. Thompson, A. Robinson, David Roberts and Charles C. Hall.

For Glossop material I am indebted to the town's public library, Glossop Heritage Centre, Jim Bennett, A.K. Kirby and the TMS. I owe a particular obligation to Greg Fox, publisher of my *Glossop Tramways* in 1991, for permission to include photographs from that work, plus his plan of the tramway system.

Finally, the Matlock section has been enhanced by views provided by David Nutt, the Arkwright Society, the Derbyshire Library Service, Glynn Waite and the Science Museum, London. To all who have assisted in the compilation of this real labour of love I offer my heartiest gratitude and appreciation.

Introduction

In the tramway heyday, no less than seven systems operated in the county of Derbyshire, including horse cars, electric cars and cable cars. Tramcars ran within towns and along inter-urban networks. The Ashby & Burton Light Railway was a true light railway since it was constructed in 1906 by the Midland Railway as an alternative to a standard railway line, and though it crossed south Derbyshire from west to east, with a depot at Swadlincote, the two termini were at Burton-upon-Trent in Staffordshire and Ashby-de-la-Zouch in Leicestershire. Similarly the Nottinghamshire & Derbyshire Tramway, a latecomer to the scene in 1913, ran between Ripley in Derbyshire and the city of Nottingham, though the line was merely the emasculated remnant of a much larger enterprise.

The earliest tramways in Derbyshire were horse car systems run by the Derby Tramways Company from 1880 to 1899, when the Corporation took over, and by two successive private companies in Chesterfield which opened in 1882, before another municipal takeover, again in 1899. In the meantime, in 1893, Sir George Newnes, a publishing magnate born in Matlock, financed a half-mile cable tramway in his native township, which ran up a steep one-in-five bank. In 1898 Newnes bought out the other shareholders, and presented it to the Matlock UDC as a gift. It ran as a local facility for nearly thirty more years.

The first electric tramway to run in Derbyshire commenced operations in the unlikely venue of Ilkeston, and was another Corporation funded enterprise. After a late start due to the inefficiency of the electricity supplier, the first electric car ran in May 1903. Hard on its heels came another system in the equally unexpected and isolated township of Glossop, which opened for business in August of the same year. This undertaking was financed by the Urban Electricity Supply Company, which owned another tramway in Cornwall, and also provided electricity for the locality.

Derby Corporation opened its own electric tramway in July 1904, replacing its horse car fleet, and extending its tracks to cover eight routes which radiated outwards from the town centre. Chesterfield followed Derby's lead in electrifying its own diminutive horse car line and extending it through the town centre northwards in December 1904. The Burton & Ashby inter-urban first operated in June 1906 and the Notts & Derby line, the final system to begin operations in Derbyshire, commenced running in July 1913. Sadly, none of the electric car undertakings lived long enough to celebrate their thirtieth birthdays, though Matlock's cable fleet survived for thirty-four years. The loans for the trams, overhead wires and track were taken out over long periods with little thought for depreciation, and the smaller enterprises found their equipment ageing and passenger receipts generally too low to sustain them, a circumstance exacerbated by the First World War, which brought shortages of materials and a heavy drain on resources.

By the end of the war heavy outlays were necessary for replacing tramway components, and both councils and companies began seeking alternative and cheaper transport options. A spate of Derbyshire tramway closures commenced in 1927, with Burton & Ashby in the van in February, followed closely by Chesterfield who replaced their tramcars with trolleybuses in May. Matlock followed suit in September and Glossop in December, both authorities substituting motorbuses for their trams. Ilkeston soldiered on until February 1931 before, having been taken over by Notts & Derby in 1916, converting to trolleybuses and linking up with their sister enterprise. The latter ceased tramcar services in 1932, after only twenty-one years, and likewise introduced railless vehicles. Only Derby remained as a tram stronghold, but by 1934 the county town too had adopted trackless vehicles, and the thirty-one year reign of the electric tramcar in Derbyshire was at an end.

This volume will concentrate on the north Derbyshire undertakings of Chesterfield, Glossop and Matlock, with the intention of covering the southern Derbyshire systems in a subsequent volume.

Barry M. Marsden
Eldwick, April 2002

One
The Chesterfield Horse Tramways (1882-1904)

The foundations of public transport in Chesterfield date from October 1878 when the first proposals for a public horse tramway were placed before the Town Council by Edward Nicholls of Brampton Manor. Due to local disagreements and difficulties it took some time for the promoters to realize their plans for opening any of their suggested routes. In fact the first rails were not laid until 1882 and then only one part of the proposed tramway, from Walton Lane, Brampton, to Low Pavement, by the Market Place, was actually constructed. It was laid on a gauge of 4ft 8½in, as a single track with four passing loops, and was a diminutive one and a quarter miles in length. A tramshed was erected in Rodney Yard, and the first car had its trial run on 5 October 1882, almost four years after the original proposals had been first mooted. The Low Pavement-Walton run was finally opened for traffic one month later, on 8 November.

The promoters of the enterprise formed a company, the Chesterfield & District Tramways Company, registered in December 1881 with a capital of £30,000. The original fleet comprised three vehicles, all built by Ashbury's of Manchester, and a stud of twelve horses. Cars 1 and 2 were double-deckers pulled by a pair of horses, and were both built on Eade's patent reversible trucks. This design allowed the car body to swivel through 180 degrees, pulled round by side-stepping horses, so that at the two termini there was no need to unharness the animals, thus saving time and manpower. Both cars had a single staircase at the rear, with seating for thirty-two, sixteen on each deck. The third tram was a one-horse single-decker with seats for sixteen.

The tramway was soon beset by problems and difficulties, and apparently little could be said in its favour. The general operation was deficient, its timekeeping unimpressive, and there was a lack of competent staff. It 'was in every way unreliable' according to the local press. Financial pressures plagued the undertaking during its short life, and it went into voluntary liquidation three years to the month it first commenced operations. A new company, the Chesterfield Tramways Company, consisting of twelve local businessmen, purchased the defunct facility on 6 December 1886 for the sum of £1,050, a shrewd bargain as the total debts were only £445. Only five of the original horses remained, and for the rest of its life as a private company, the number of horses never rose above eight. In 1890 the company increased their rolling stock by purchasing two additional small cars, numbers 4 and 5, both sixteen seat one-horse single-deckers built by Milnes of Hadley.

Chesterfield Corporation, following the lead of other nearby municipalities such as Sheffield, set up a sub-committee in 1897 to discuss terms for purchasing the tramway. The company sensibly expressed their willingness to sell out for £2,000, but an over-generous council actually paid them £2,050, and the takeover was finalized on 22 November of that year. A Tramways sub-committee was set up, and doubtless to the delight of the travelling public, the fares were reduced from 2d to 1d. Though receipts naturally rose, so did overloading, with subsequent requests for increases in the frequency of the service. A further sixteen-seat car (No.6) built by Milnes, was delivered in April 1898, at a cost of £125, followed by two others of the same type (Nos 7 and 8), which arrived a year later. Half a million tram tickets were purchased in 1897 at a cost of £9 7s 6d. As a local firm paid £10 for the advertising rights on the same tickets, the Corporation made a useful profit on the deal! In 1898 Eyre & Sons' tender of £16 for advertising on the cars and stable for twelve months was accepted, and in 1901 Thomas Spencer paid 10 guineas to advertise on 500,000 tram tickets. In January 1904 500,000 1d tickets and 50,000 halfpenny tickets went to tender for similar rights. Incidentally, tram conductors started each day with £1 in small denomination coinage. Passengers placed their fares in special boxes fixed to each car, the conductor providing them with any necessary change. Tickets were issued from a roll, and for some years the cash boxes were emptied by a firm of local accountants, rather than the tramway staff!

Under Corporation management the tramway prospered, and it was decided to repaint all the vehicles in 1899. The colour scheme was Prussian blue and primrose, with a white roof. None of the staff were ever provided with uniforms, despite more than one petition; the only uniform provided was for the inspector, Frank Root, who received his first example in January 1900. By 1902 the line was wearing out, and the tracks were in need of much repair. Decisions on electrification were in the pipeline, but the increased traffic led to a decision to purchase one second-hand two-decker (not two as has often been stated) from nearby Sheffield. The tram was duly acquired, at the knock-down price of £5, but whether the heavy vehicle ever actually operated on the decrepit rails of the town is another matter.

By 1904 the horse car track was on its last legs, the Tramway Manager Robert Acland reporting that it was 'practically worn out, and in many places a source of danger to light wheeled vehicles using the road.' By June 1904 the Chesterfield Corporation Tramways and Improvements Act had received the Royal Assent, and in August the old rails had been lifted and a new tramtrack for the electric cars was in the process of being laid. By the end of September the line and loop track was in position from the Market Place to the Old Pheasant Inn on the western boundary of the borough, well beyond the old horse car terminus at Walton Lane. The horse trams, which had come under the authority of the Electric Tramways Committee from 1 July, obviously had to cease operations during the new construction work, but they enjoyed a final swansong, with five of them working the route over the new smooth-running rails for nearly three months and appearing in several photographs alongside their brand-new replacements. They then passed into honourable retirement, and only Car 8 has survived for posterity.

Overleaf: Edward Nicholls formed the Chesterfield & District Tramways Company in 1881 with a capital of £30,000. The proposed lines are shown on his plan, drawn by his engineer Charles H. Beloe, but only one – the Market Hall to Walton Lane stretch – was ever completed. This opened for service in November 1882.

This view of the north side of Chesterfield Market Place and its busy throng almost certainly dates to the opening of the horse tramway in 1882. Schofield's glass and ceramic shop, to the right of T.P. Wood's wine and spirit merchants, did not yield to J. White's music emporium until the late 1890s, and the garlanded poles are certainly not electric traction poles. They are too thin, and in the wrong places.

A unique view of one of the 5-6 class of Milnes single-deckers supplied to the tramway in 1890, standing at the Low Pavement terminus. Note that the turtleback roof has no clerestory windows, unlike the later 7-8 examples, and the side windows are squareheaded. Colours are unknown, but the fancy lining-out includes the fleet number 5 in a garter. The company name is likewise ornately rendered, and Eyre's furnishers have the advertising rights on the cars.

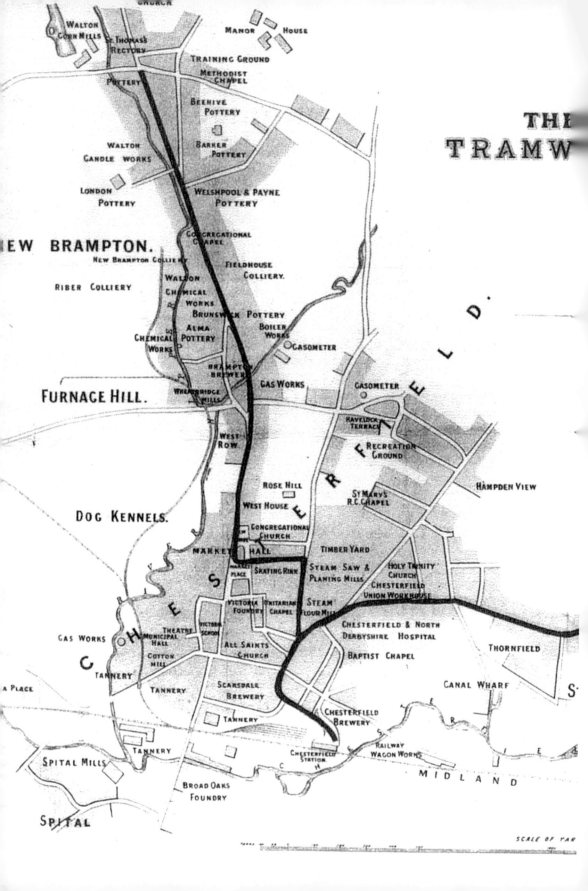

CHESTERFIELD · & · DISTRICT
YS · COMPANY, · LIMITED.

LINES PROPOSED TO BE CONSTRUCTED SHEWN THUS ▬▬▬

Charles H. Beloe.
M. Inst C. E.
13, Harrington Street,
LIVERPOOL.

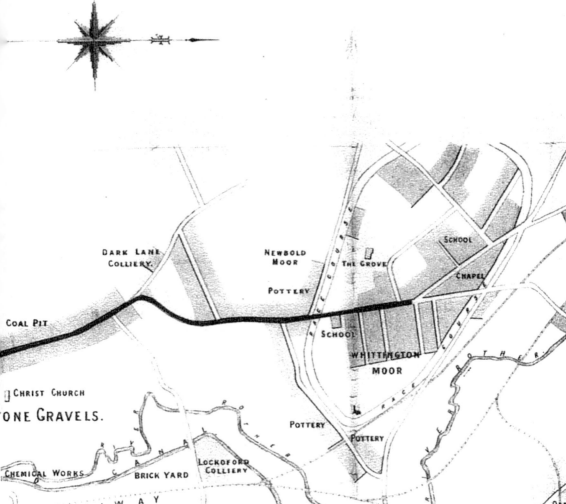

DARK LANE
COLLIERY.

NEWBOLD
MOOR

THE GROVE

SCHOOL

CHAPEL

POTTERY

COAL PIT

SCHOOL

WHITTINGTON

MOOR

CHRIST CHURCH

ONE GRAVELS.

POTTERY

POTTERY

CHEMICAL WORKS

BRICK YARD

LOCKOFORD
COLLIERY

FOX

OAKS C

R A I L W A Y

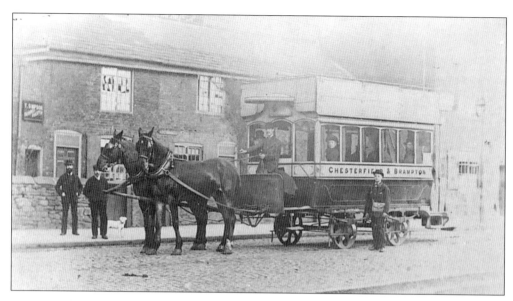

This may be the earliest shot of an Eade's two-decker, posing on West Bars with a youthful conductor obscuring the fleet number. Note the lining-out on the rocker panel, which closely parallels that on Car 5, suggesting that the dating is pre-1897 before the Corporation takeover of the line. The Square and Compass public house can be seen behind the single staircase on the extreme right.

A dire print, but of some significance, as it shows the horse tram crews in the Rodney Yard Depot in early 1900. Inspector Francis Root was granted a uniform at this time, and he can be seen on the back row in front of a line-up of 6-8 class cars. Second from left on the back row is Seth Hall, and second left front row his son Horace. Both later became electric tram motormen. The dapper gent in the bowler is driver Ezra Coates.

Horse Car 2 pictured turning at the Market Place terminus in the early 1900s. The side-stepping horses are swinging the car body round the axis of the rigid truck for the journey to Walton Lane.

A fine study of Eade's two-decker No.1 proceeding at some 2mph along Chatsworth Road towards Brampton c.1900. Note the splendidly nonchalant driver, and the Mason's Arms public house on the right. This locality is still recognizable after some 100 years.

Eade's Car 2, with yet another juvenile conductor, pauses at the Walton Lane terminus around
the same date. The twin-track termination can be seen behind the rear hoofs of the horses.

An interesting rear view of one of the two-deckers approaching the Market Place, with the old
Sun Inn on the left, and the brand-new Portland Hotel opposite. The details of the curved
staircase and upper deck knifeboard seating show up well.

Horse Car 8, now preserved at Crich Tramway Museum, poses at Low Pavement, drawn by a pair of horses. Ezra Coates, later a stalwart on the electric cars, is the driver, but the young heavily laden conductor is unknown. The view provides interesting details of the car body and exterior fitments.

Another good view of Eade's Car 1 about to depart from the Market Hall terminus on market day around 1902. An interested cluster of youngsters survey the camera from a respectful distance, and the details of the patent trucks are well defined.

Single-deck Car 7 shows off its salient points in afternoon sunshine at the same spot as the previous view. Note the curtained interior of the saloon, and the principal town centre shops visible in the background. The driver is Seth Hall, the conductor his son Horace.

Horse Car 8 passes an unidentified single-decker on the loop in a surprisingly leafy West Bars around 1903. Road and track are in an appalling state, and cars often derailed and re-engaged the tram groove further on. Steps to electrify the fleet were already in the pipeline.

Horse Tram 8 in single harness and muddy condition at rest for the camera on a filthy stretch of road, almost certainly in the last winter of the service. The driver is again Ezra Coates, and the view is taken along West Bars, with Clarence Road on the right.

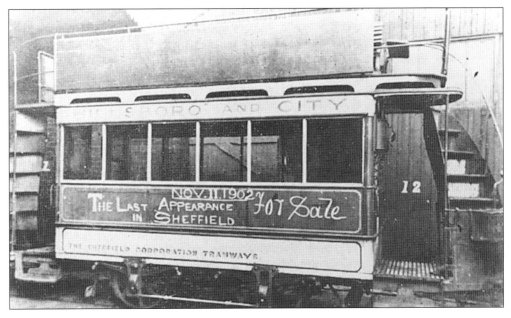

The Tramways Committee had been seeking a second-hand two-decker to supplement the fleet, and the clumsy Heath-Robinson vehicle shown, Sheffield's Hillsborough 47, may be the very one chosen. Certainly a Sheffield car was purchased early in 1903 at the knockdown price of £5! Whether it actually operated on the decrepit rails of the town is another matter.

Horse Car 8 was sold off as a summerhouse in early 1905, but was rescued by Philip Robinson, Chairman of the Tramways/Transport Committee, in 1934. This photograph shows the tram in the depot yard at Thornfield standing in front of the crew's rest room. The tram was later restored, but endured a chequered career before its removal to Crich in the 1980s.

Two
Chesterfield Corporation Tramways –
Tracklaying and Trials (1904)

Robert Lawford Acland, Borough Electrical Engineer, was the driving force behind the formulation, planning and execution of the electric tramways policy. He prepared a series of reports on the electrification of the line, suggesting its extension to the borough boundary on the west, then through the town centre to Whittington Moor as far as the New Inn, a distance of just under four miles. In 1903 he costed out the whole operation, including tracklaying, overhead and electric cars at £55,714, allowing for a single track and turnout arrangement, with double lines through town from New Square to the Sheffield-Newbold Road junction. The Chesterfield Corporation Tramways and Improvements Act received Royal assent on 24 June 1904 and the contract for track and overhead was awarded to British Insulated & Helsby Cables, stipulating completion within five months.

The line began at the western borough boundary at the Old Pheasant Inn, and was laid as single track, central to the road, running as far as Low Pavement and embodying seven passing loops. The overhead utilized twin poles and span wire. The through-town line was double track, with a facing crossover in Cavendish Street, using mainly bracket poles to carry the running wire. From the Sheffield-Newbold Road junction the track was again single line, with six turnouts, and carried bracket poles throughout owing to the GPO telephone lines on this part of the route. Final amendments included the abandonment of the last stretch of the line to the New Inn, the track terminating at the Whittington UDC boundary at Duke Street, and measuring a total length of 3.58 miles.

Some aspects of the planned route were questioned, including the western extension to the Old Pheasant Inn, but Acland believed this would encourage housing growth along Chatsworth Road, and create evening and weekend passenger traffic out into the countryside. The double track through the narrow town centre also came under fire, but the manager justified it by claiming that a single line would create even more problems by impeding the traffic flow. The first symbolic excavation of the road took place at the Old Pheasant on 8 August, and a local workforce of some 200-250 men began operations there, and at the Sheffield-Newbold Road junction, the latter pushing towards Whittington. Serious dislocation of urban traffic was immediate, leading to much inconvenience, especially when the through-town tracks were laid in mid-October. The Whittington UDCs were swift to condemn the contractors for blocking roads, dumping spoil indiscriminately, and proceeding with 'total indifference and careless disregard' for the public.

Matters came to a head in the town centre when a promise to lay the lines in two weeks dragged out into more than eight. The town councillors, (some of whom glibly criticised the workmen), the local press, shopkeepers and businesses (whose takings fell by 50%) and the contractors all came into conflict, and matters were not helped by continuing bad weather which turned the streets into quagmires. By working at night with arc lamps, British Helsby eventually completed the job by late November, the rails lying on a nine-inch concrete bed, and with woodblock setts carried through the mid-town thoroughfares.

The tramcars themselves, supplied by the Brush Company of Loughborough, and neatly painted in a livery of Carmine and Primrose, were standard two-deckers of the 'Preston' type, but were mounted on state-of-the-art Radial trucks, designed by Lycett & Conaty. These were designed to give some flexibility on curves as opposed to the normal rigid trucks of the period, and with an 8ft 6in wheelbase, were some 2ft longer than normal trucks, ensuring a steadier ride, with no pitching 'end rock' and giving easier negotiation of bends and when running through points. Chesterfield was the first town to completely equip cars with radial trucks, which was a brave move, as faults could easily develop with an untried piece of mechanism.

The struck-down electric cars began arriving at the newly built tramshed on Chatsworth Road in late November and were shipped along the sidings of the Midland Railway as far as Factory Street, where horse-drawn low loaders conveyed them to the depot for fitting together. Car 6 was among the first to be constructed, though it was No.9, driven by Acland himself, which took part in the first trial run on 3 December, from the Old Pheasant to West Bars, the only part of the line then complete. Car 7, a fleet favourite with photographers throughout its life, took part in further trials on the 7th and 9th of the month, and both trams posed alongside horse cars for posterity. The Market Place to Brampton line was ready for business in late December, and the first service car ran this route on Tuesday the 20th, ferrying some 3,298 passengers by the end of that day. The Cavendish Street to Jug and Glass section opened on Christmas Eve, and the whole track became fully operational as far as the Whittington terminus six days later.

Opposite page: The narrow confines of Burlington Street look decidedly unpromising for the laying out of a double tramline as this busy 1900 panorama suggests. There was the added problem of a sharp left-hand turn at the far end of the thoroughfare, beneath the Crooked Spire visible in the distance. However, twin track was laid in October-November 1904, though at weekends the through-town line was abandoned, due to the shoppers thronging the locality.

Right: Robert Lawford Acland was responsible for planning and organizing the Chesterfield electricity and electric tramway enterprises. He became tramways manager in 1904 and served the Corporation with distinction until his resignation in 1919 to join the Metropolitan Electricity Company at Uxbridge.

Left: Sir Ernest Shentall was chairman of the Tramways Committee from 1904 to 1920, and a committee member thereafter. A strong supporter of the tramway, he became an inveterate opponent of the policy of trolleybus replacement of the trams in the mid-1920s.

Local photographer Charles Nadin was active with his camera during the intensive tracklaying operations of Autumn 1904. This shot, dated 23 October, shows camera-conscious bystanders, including an inquisitive postman, surveying the work on a thoroughly disrupted High Street. The bracket poles are already *in situ*, but the overhead wires have not yet been strung.

Further along in Burlington Street and looking in the opposite direction, the laying of the rails continues, causing short-term chaos to traffic and local businesses. Here the traction poles have their bowstrings in position, though not the running wire.

Right: This view of New Square, looking east towards High Street, shows the laying of the double line under the windows of the Market Hall Coffee Rooms. In the distance the poles for the span wire have already been erected.

Below: This scene, on the sharp Burlington Street curve, looking towards Cavendish Street, shows the hectic activity associated with the laying of the rails, with a venturesome lady giving a fresh meaning to walking the plank! Only the buildings on the left retain their 1904 frontages.

LAYING THE ELECTRIC TRAMWAY CHESTERFIELD

Under the gaze of interested spectators, the workforce busy themselves with laying the Cavendish Street facing crossover, for use at weekends as a terminus when the through-town line was closed.

The crossover under construction along Cavendish Street on a sunny winter day. Note the complicated trackwork associated with the line, and the somewhat dandified bystanders proving how interesting it is to watch less fortunate mortals dirty their hands!

Cavendish Street looking towards Holywell Cross at an earlier stage in the proceedings, with bemused passers-by witnessing the road surface being hacked up and excavated to a considerable depth. The frontages have changed considerably since this view was taken.

A first-rate official British Helsby photograph of the tracklaying at the southern end of Sheffield Road in August 1904, with the layout of the Holy Trinity Church passing loop clearly shown. Note the stone setts on the right, and the motley group of navvies and onlookers.

A more wintery scene than the last at the same venue, though looking in the opposite direction. Here the through-town rails have just been joined to the Sheffield Road tracks by Holywell House on the right. A policeman tries to bring order to chaos as the blocked road obviously necessitated a detour to Whittington via Newbold Road on the left.

Another official British Helsby view, this time of the 'Y' track layout at the entrance to the tram depot. This work was in progress in mid-October, and the usual sightseers have materialized to hamper the workforce.

Another picture of the junction, showing the tracks curving out of the depot, and crossing the lengthy turnout which took cars to Brampton and town. Again an officer of the law controls the spectators, and the man on the right is probably explaining to his baby-in-arms the many benefits the new undertaking will bring.

Chatsworth Road looking townward, a fine study of the layout of the passing loop outside the tramshed with the 'Y' junction visible in the near distance. Local traffic must have been at a standstill throughout the construction of this part of the line.

Tracklaying began on 8 August at the Old Pheasant. Here, the single line running by St Thomas's Church on Chatsworth Road is flanked by piled-up spoil on one side, and a narrow length of roadway on the other, almost totally blocking the thoroughfare.

ARRIVAL OF NEW ELECTRIC CAR CHESTERFIELD NOV. 30 1904

Nadin recorded a significant piece of local transport history when he photographed the body of Car 10, mounted in pristine splendour on a horse-drawn low-loader outside the new tram depot on 30 November 1904. Again the local law oversees proceedings. The overhead is being strung; note the drum on the left, which contained half a mile of hard drawn copper wire.

The following three views mark the arrival of Car 7 at the depot. Here, the tram body is being manoeuvred on to Chatsworth Road from the Factory Street railway siding, with the Barrel Inn in the background. The running wire is in position here, and the track laid, though the dreadful state of the road makes the latter hard to believe!

The first in a series of the 'Old and New Car' theme picks Horse Car 8 and Electric Car 7 posed together by the refreshment room opposite the tram depot.

31

NEW ELECTRIC CAR CHESTERFIELD

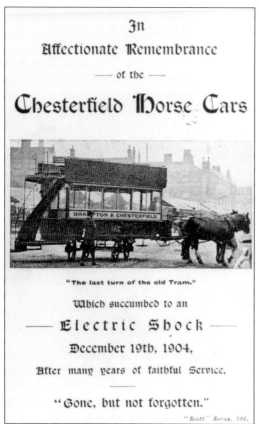

In

Affectionate Remembrance

—— of the ——

Chesterfield Horse Cars

"The last turn of the old Tram."

Which succumbed to an

—— Electric Shock ——

December 19th, 1904,

After many years of faithful Service,

"Gone, but not forgotten."

"Scott" Series, 346.

Above: At rest in the depot yard, the body of Car 7 awaits unloading and the fitting together of the component parts. The photograph gives a good sight of the already applied livery. Note the fairly discreet Brush Company advertising bill in the saloon window.

Left: The Scott Postcard Company must have made a significant profit in retailing cards, first lamenting the demise of the horse tram networks, then celebrating the nation's new electric trams. Here the passing of the Chesterfield system is suitably marked by the picture of Eade's Car 2 turning on Low Pavement.

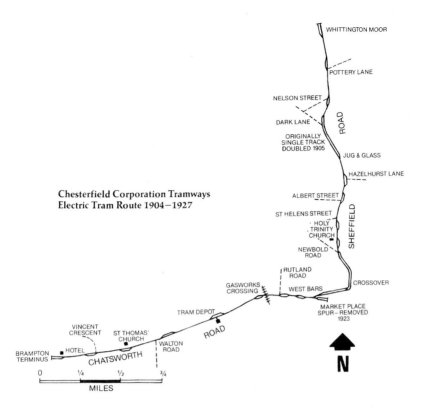

Chesterfield Corporation Tramways
Electric Tram Route 1904–1927

WHITTINGTON MOOR

POTTERY LANE

NELSON STREET

DARK LANE

ORIGINALLY
SINGLE TRACK
DOUBLED 1905

JUG & GLASS

HAZELHURST LANE

ALBERT STREET

ST HELENS STREET

HOLY
TRINITY
CHURCH

NEWBOLD
ROAD

RUTLAND
ROAD

GASWORKS
CROSSING

WEST BARS

CROSSOVER

MARKET PLACE
SPUR – REMOVED
1923

TRAM DEPOT

VINCENT
CRESCENT

ST THOMAS'
CHURCH

WALTON
ROAD

BRAMPTON
TERMINUS

HOTEL

CHATSWORTH ROAD

N

0   ¼   ½   ¾

MILES

The tramline as completed formed a reversed 'L', with open-ended sections of twin track at both termini. In 1905 the line between the Jug and Glass and Dark Lane was doubled. Though it was proposed to double the Holy Trinity-Jug and Glass section, this was never implemented.

Right: Acland chose the state-of-the-art Radial truck for his electric cars, as it gave a smoother ride with greater flexibility on curves than the standard rigid trucks then in service. Here one of the newfangled items can be seen on a Brush Company traverser.

33

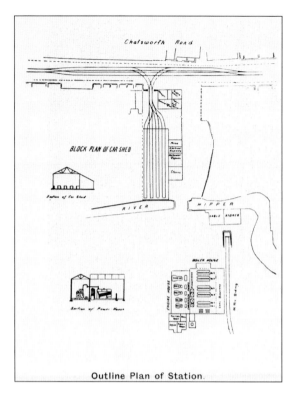

Chatsworth Road

BLOCK PLAN OF CAR SHED

Section of Car Shed

RIVER

Section of Power House

Outline Plan of Station.

Left: The layout of the new tram depot and its associated trackwork can be seen in this 1904 plan of the premises. The tramshed was extended on the western side in 1914 to accommodate the three new 16-18 class covered top cars.

Below: The tramshed, built of brick with a slate roof, measured 120ft by 46ft, and was intended to hold sixteen cars in four tracks set over inspection pits. Note the tower wagon parked on the left.

Opposite below: Brand-new Car 6, photographed in the depot yard shortly after completion. Of particular interest is the patent brass bar fitted to the front platform. Raising the bar lowered the folding step below the platform for passenger access. Lowering the bar lifted the step to the position seen in the view.

A splendid shot of the newly arrived tramcars in the shed built to receive them. Car 9 is fully assembled, apart from the upper deck wire mesh. No.6 sports the netting, but has no lifeguards, while Cars 7 and 8 are still in the process of construction. Note the line of trolley masts along the wall on the left of the carshed.

Charles Nadin was present to record the first electric car trial at Brampton terminus on 3 December 1904 in the presence of Brush Company officials. Robert Acland mans the controls, while the lady on his left, holding a small child, is evidently his wife. The Old Pheasant Inn, pulled down in 1906, can be seen to the right of the tram.

Another Scott money-spinner was the 'Old and New Car' theme, exploited in this postcard of Car 9, on its initial trial, meeting Horse Car 7 on the turnout by the tram depot on another swampy stretch of main road.

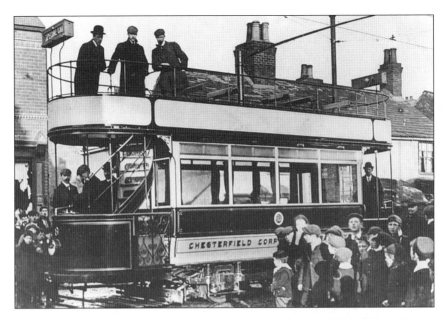

Acland fiddles with the controls as Car 9 rests in front of School Board Lane, elegant in its new livery. Note the wrought iron gate between the dash panel and the body, and the fancy scrollwork in the angle above. The coat-of-arms and lettering in the rocker panel show up well. This scene was evidently recorded at lunchtime, and features the inquisitive children from the nearby Brampton Board School.

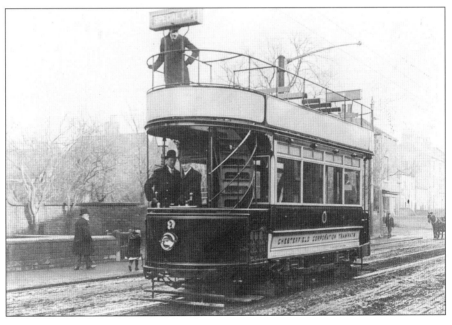

Further along Chatsworth Road Car 9 pauses for another photo call, though the old gentleman on the left seems singularly unimpressed by the example of progress passing by.

Another trial later the same week reveals the system's favourite vehicle, Car 7, posed close by the spot occupied by No.9 in the previous picture. On the platform, and wearing his horse car uniform, is Inspector Root, presumably by this time confirmed as the new Chief Inspector of the electric tramway.

The old and new car theme is again exploited as Ezra Coates' Horse Car 8 meets Electric Car 7 on the St Thomas's loop, opposite Stewart's tailors, then at 480 Chatsworth Road. Inspector Root stands by the side of the latter, and the lineup is completed by a curious postman.

The Scott Company scored again, with this card marking the appearance of the new transport facility in Chesterfield, unusual in that it portrays an actual location, at the top of the Market Place. This example is fairly restrained, as some are a little more risqué!

An excellent side-on study taken at Brampton terminus in early February 1905, neatly dated by the window bill advertising that week's offering, *The Ladder of Life*, at the grandiosely named Theatre Royal, later the more prosaic Hippodrome. The wrought iron gate has a tinplate sign affixed, and the radial truck and magnetic brake show up well.

Taken from a coloured postcard dating from the winter of 1904-1905 Car 7, gleaming in its new paint job and driven by Motorman Marshall, is caught by the camera in the sylvan surroundings of the Brampton terminus. The margins of the road are in an appalling state.

Three
The Electric Trams –
Early Years (1904-1914)

The electric tramcars quickly became an accepted feature of the town, providing a fairly swift and efficient service for the population. There were early teething troubles, especially with the timetable; in March 1905 locals petitioned against the unsatisfactory working of the line, with cars at Walton Road often arriving 15 minutes late 'to the great annoyance and inconvenience of passengers'. Since the vehicles had been running some three months, ran the complaint 'it surely is time that something like regularity and punctuality was observed.' There were also problems with the laying of the setts at the Brampton end of the facility, which necessitated contact with British Helsby in early 1906.

Accidents were of course endemic to any transport system, and Chesterfield was no exception. The most bizarre early one occurred in September 1905 when two cars managed a head-on collision on single line near Nelson Street in broad daylight. Apparently one motorman was too busy watching a football match in a field adjoining the road to notice his oncoming opposite number! The following month another tram helped a motor car into a butcher's shop at Stonegravels, and in June 1906 Car 6 pushed a coal cart into a wall by the Jug and Glass. Horse and traps were the favourite prey of the Chesterfield motormen and dozens of these were damaged by careless driving during the life of the system.

Advertising on the trams was contracted to one A.C. Burnley in the early years, but his reluctance to pay his bills led to much litigation, and he was eventually discarded in favour of a more reliable client, Griffiths & Millington, who subsequently held the rights for many years. In 1906 tram crew uniform issues were standardized at one set per year, plus one overcoat every two years. In September of that year the Hasland Parish Council urged the extension of the tramway to their locality and to Birdholme on Derby Road, as projected in the 1904 Tramways Bill, but the Corporation felt unable to proceed with the projected lines at that time; in fact they never did. In January 1907 electric clocks were provided at each terminus, and in May, following a decision of September 1906, the Town Clerk negotiated a loan of £2,000 for the purchase of two additional vehicles from the Brush Company. They arrived in September, the cars costing £748 and the electrical equipment £515. Interestingly enough the trucks were of the Brush Flexible Axle type, a rigid four wheel version, with limited play on the axles. A darkish shot of one tram shows semi-elliptical springs under each axlebox, a feature of the later Brush Long Wheelbase design. Later photographs of these cars, which were numbered 13 and 14, show different axlebox layouts, and it may be that the trams were re-trucked at some stage.

In September 1908 Acland ordered a water car from Brush. The little service tram (given the number 15), arrived in February 1909 and cost £744. It was a versatile addition to the fleet, being capable of watering the whole route with its 2,000 gallon capacity tank, and also had the ability to flush drains and wash down the Market Square with its fire hydrants. Its rail-flushing nozzles were highly efficient, and in winter it could function as a snowplough. It was perhaps too effective in this role, as the Newbold and Whittington UDCs complained vehemently each winter that the car simply pushed the accumulated snow off the rails, and dumped it on either side of the permanent way, thereby blocking off the road!

The wear on the track had assumed serious proportions, as in August 1909 a portable rail grinder was purchased to remove corrugations on the line. Track wear had been remarked on by Acland some time previously, especially at the entrances to curves. The jarring experienced by cars when entering loops was accentuated by the type of points utilized. The problem could only get worse, and track expenditure began to rise from 1908 onwards. By 1910, while tramway outlay was rising, income remained virtually static, and the expedient of lowering fares was tried in an effort to stimulate traffic. The opportunity to try out the idea occurred during the eight-day shopping festival in September. Passenger numbers increased by 17,646 during the period, but receipts grew by only £28! A decorated and illuminated tram was adorned to celebrate the event, but the expense of be-draping the conveyance had to be shouldered by the electricity department at a cost of £25. A modest wage rise asked for by the traffic staff in November, in line with general wages in the industry, was refused as the previous year tramway profits had been a mere £25, without allowing for depreciation.

In December 1910 the practicability of top-covering the tram fleet was discussed. Acland preferred scheduling extra cars in bad weather, but often passengers tended to overcrowd the first one to arrive, leaving the following cars empty. A survey carried out in January 1911 purported to prove that the travelling public enjoyed freezing on the uncovered tops of trams, but what other option was available if the lower saloon was full? Considering that nearly every other tramway system had top-covered at least part of their rolling stock, Acland suggested converting four trams, but this decision was ultimately deferred.

Tramway correspondence shows a comparison of crews' wages that year, as the union had raised the question of finance. In 1905 a motorman's pay had been £1 3s 2d per week (4½d an hour). By 1911 it was £1 11s 4d (6d an hour), with conductors earning some 5s a week less. In November the staff were granted seven days' yearly holiday with pay, as against a previous three, and they may well have thought Utopia was nigh. However, by 1912 the staff had received no pay rise for four years, and conditions of service had deteriorated. Crews worked an average of 62½ hours a week, but whereas previously they undertook one return run from Brampton to Whittington every hour in a nine-hour stint, now ten journeys had to be fitted into the same time period. Twelve hours were worked on Sundays with no extra pay, and only six days' holiday was paid for, as against the previous seven.

In October 1913 tenders were invited for a further augmentation of the tram fleet, for three balcony top-covered vehicles, and the Brush Company was successful in its bid. The price was £469 for each body, plus £282 for the electrics and £55 for each electric track brake. To accommodate the increase in car numbers the tramshed had to be extended on its western side, and a quote of £321 was accepted for this work in January 1914. These first all-weather vehicles, which arrived in June of that year, were numbered 16 to 18. They boasted more ornate lettering on the dash panels than the earlier cars, with the Corporation coat-of-arms incorporated in a shield rather than a circle. The most important improvement however, apart from the covers, was the new Peckham Pendulum P22 truck, whose pendulum gearing allowed the axles to move laterally, independently of the truck frame and car body, so the axles could more easily adapt to irregularities in the track. The result was a smoother ride, and freedom from side oscillation. Doubtless the Corporation motormen looked forward to trying out the new mounts, and riders who had shivered on open-toppers through ten winters must have been more than happy to enjoy the luxury of enclosed top decks, though fourteen of the seventeen fleet vehicles still kept their uncovered upperworks.

Brampton terminus in 1906, the western end of the tramway. In that year the Old Pheasant Inn was demolished and replaced by the Terminus Hotel, here shown under completion. The double line, in its bed of stone setts, can be clearly seen. From here to town the overhead was carried on twin poles and span wire. The hotel was demolished in July 2002.

Electric Car 4 poses on Burlington Street on the Brampton run in late 1904, manned by Motorman Stone. Note particularly the narrow space between the nearside of the tram and the pavement. High on the right-hand wall can be seen the metal replica of an old beehive, the trademark of the Beehive Drapery shop.

This study of Car 11 heading along Sheffield Road towards Dark Lane can only have been taken between January and May 1905, the short time the line was single track. Even while the rails were being laid it was realized that twin-track was a necessity due to the sharp right-hand bend in the distance, which hid oncoming trams. A waiting car can just be seen on the extreme right of the photograph.

Above: It seems incredible that there were areas as rural as this on the tram route. This scene is just round the distant corner from the last view, with Dark Lane hidden off to the right, and shows the end of the new double track being laid from the Jug and Glass in May 1905. Acland supervises the proceedings, managing to hide the fleet number of the service car behind him as he does so. This spot is now a busy roundabout.

Previous page: Tramway staff, resplendent in new uniforms and a variety of hirsute adornment, pose in front of one of the new vehicles early in 1905. They include, top row, from left to right: W. Pickering, J. Baker, F. Root, W. Townsend, C. Davenport. Third row: B. Shaw, E. Coates, J. Cotterill, H. Bacon, E. Birks, B. Mortimer, W. Owen, J. Haw. Second row: A. Wicks, C. Hopkinson, H. Longden, C. Marshall, S. Hall, C. Stubbs, J. Stone, J. Wheatley, J. Lander. Front row: G. Woodhouse, G. Boden, D. Lowe, Jack Blount, T. Mellor, James Blount, G. Turner, E. Bennett,-?- Kirk.

This part of Chatsworth Road, with the Mason's Arms on the right, has changed little since 1905, as Car 1 waits on the gasworks loop. The Midland Railway had a line crossing the tramway into the works a little further to the right, and often delayed the service by closing the level crossing gates to allow their rolling stock to move, a great bone of contention with Acland and his staff. The junction of tram and railway track later became a notorious black spot as the rails wore and ensured a lurching ride over the joints.

Car 6 heads Bramptonwards, though the conductor has neglected to turn the indicator blind, which still reads MARKET PLACE. In this busy scene Nadin's shop is just off to the left, with the Portland Hotel on the right. The Sun Inn, centre left, has not yet had its refurbishment in 'Public Convenience' style, with singular white, cream and brown glazed tiling.

Car 1 negotiates the Low Pavement spur on a bustling Saturday when the through-route was suspended, and the line ended here. Not much has changed since Nadin recorded this scene, apart from the west frontage of the Market Hall, which was revamped in the early 1980s. The market stalls occupy the same spaces, and New Square is just as busy.

Climbing east out of New Square on to High Street, this postcard presents the unique view of three Corporation tramcars, running on a brand-new-looking double line. Despite its indicator, No.9 is on the Whittington route, and in the distance Nos 8 and 11 wait side-by-side. Rival transport in front of the Market Hall takes time off for a feed.

This card, franked August 1905, shows Car 10 coming up the New Square gradient on to High Street. An inside passenger eyes the camera, while carefully posed pedestrians stand frozen in statuesque array. The view gives good detail of the overhead at this point.

An excellent vista of High Street early in the life of the trams, as Car 7 picks its way along a crowded thoroughfare in weak sunshine on a damp day. The tram, not yet bedecked with advertising, is still evidently novel enough to warrant a second glance.

Further eastwards along Burlington Street, two cars pause together, including No.11 on the left on this confined thoroughfare. Dr Green's property, behind the trams, must have been inordinately noisy as the vehicles ground their way round the sharp bend into Cavendish Street. The house was later demolished to clear a way through to the Parish Church.

An almost unrecognizable part of the routeway, with the only clue the crossover under the wheels of Car 4 as it takes the 48ft curve into Cavendish Street. Dr Green's house can be seen immediately to the left of the tram, and Knifesmithgate, identified by the street name on the left, is now part of Stephenson Place.

Car 8, Whittington bound, waits on the Cavendish Street stop in the summer of 1905, a date established by the sale notices on the 'City Hall', demolished that year and replaced by a bank in 1906. Note the neatly dressed juveniles, all in clogs, and the fine ornate lamps outside the shop.

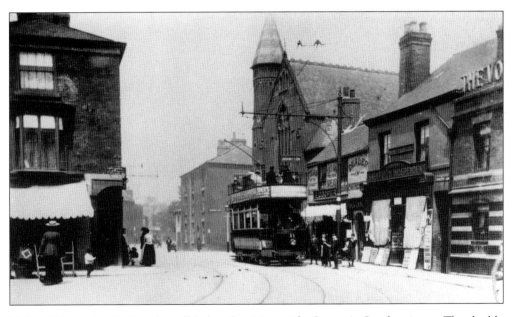

Holywell Cross in 1905 with well-laden Car 11 outside Cooper's Confectioners. The double track curves left here into Holywell Street where another tram can just be picked out in the distance. Note the complete absence of other traffic, though passing horses have left their calling cards!

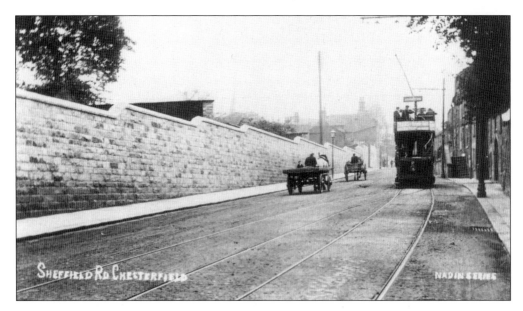

Car 2 mounts the incline above the Holy Trinity loop, heading towards the Sheffield-Newbold Road junction and town. The well-built wall on the left replaced a ramshackle one supplanted around 1910 as a frontage to the new girls' grammar school.

In this view Car 6 embarks passengers waiting on the St. Helen's Street turnout outside Day's fancy goods store at Stonegravels in 1905, while workmen clean out the points in the foreground. There are claims that the photograph was taken in December 1904, before the Whittington service became operational, but the trees, in full leaf, suggest a summer date.

Not the finest of prints, but worth reproducing as a tramscape of the Whittington end of Sheffield Road, with Car 10 moving along the single line towards town and the wall of the local school on the right. Motorman Cotterill caused the first accident on the system here on a March night in 1905 when he rammed two horse-drawn railway drays. Fortunately there were no serious injuries in the incident.

In the distance Car 7 leaves the Whittington terminus accompanied by a coal cart and horse and trap. Despite the 'Central Motor Garage' sign on the left, no motor vehicles are in evidence. At this point the single track is well to the right-hand side of the road.

A very early service picture of Car 7 posed by the drystone wall at the Brampton terminus, a favourite venue for photographers. Although the building behind is obscured by the vehicle, it can be identified as the Old Pheasant Inn, which was demolished in 1906 to make room for the Terminus Hotel. Both crewmen sport the kepi-style headgear which was provided early that year.

At the Brampton terminus at a later date, Car 4 stands by the drystone wall with the aptly named Terminus Hotel on the left, behind the refreshment kiosk. The track ended at both termini in a double, open-ended line on which trams could stand side-by-side. Note the time clock, fitted in 1907 to the standard on the right.

A fine side view of Car 4 by the wall featured in the earlier shots. Again, the patent brass bar shows up well. The motorman is Cyril Hopkinson, the conductor Derward Lowe. The day is apparently breezy, as the top deck rider is firmly holding his hat in place.

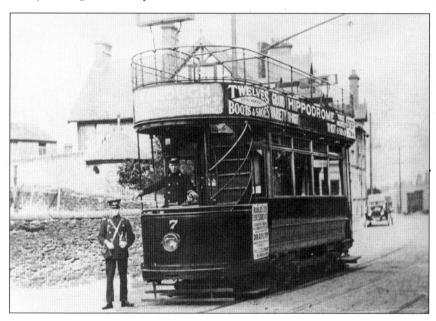

In this 1910 vista, Car 7 hides the Terminus Hotel, while an early automobile can be seen behind the tram. The motorman is Edwin Bennett, later an Inspector, who died at the early age of thirty-seven. The conductor is my namesake, though no relation.

Car 5 was rarely photographed during its service life. Here it is caught at Whittington Moor terminus on a wet, muddy day, outside Shentall's Cash Stores, owned at that time by the Chairman of the Tramways Committee. The usual assortment of bystanders keep it company.

Car 11 approaches the end of the Whittington line, with the usual crowd of urchins and others all anxious to appear in shot. The overhead, carried here on twin poles and span wire, shows up well against the skyline.

The almost inevitable Car 7 waits on the double line in this 1906 vista, again displaying the muddied thoroughfares so typical of the times. The fine bracket pole, with its ornate scrolling, was later replaced by twin standards and span wire. Behind the tram is the Black Horse Inn, and on the left Sheffield Road curves into the distance along the route the tramway was originally planned to go.

In the original scheme the tramway system was intended to run some 500 yards further along Sheffield Road on the left, terminating at the New Inn and its junction with Brimington Road, where there was an expectation of picking up the miners working at Sheepbridge Colliery. In the event the line stopped just below Duke Street on the Whittington UDC boundary, and despite promises, never penetrated further.

In 1910 a specially decorated and illuminated tram, one of the 13-14 series, and liberally studded with coloured light bulbs, helped to promote the eight day September Shopping Festival. Here the car poses for posterity on West Bars, with a service car just visible behind.

Above: A splendid study of the illuminated car aglow in the depot yard, with its crew alongside. The Electrical Energy Department fitted out the conveyance in lit-up mode at a cost of £25.

Opposite: A frontal shot of Car 9 at Whittington, with building work visible on the right. Note the clumsy and oversized destination box poised over the top deck. These were not dispensed with until after the First World War.

59

A well-thronged New Square with Tram 14 on the Low Pavement spur, indicating that the day is a Saturday. The car, indicator box showing MARKET PLACE, was added to the fleet in 1907. Here the main track curves to the left, following the line of the road.

A good view of Service Car 15 on the Brush traverser, shown without electrics, but with a snowplough fixed to the near end. The vehicle boasted a Brush long wheel base truck, which shows up clearly in the picture. This little tram cost £744 when purchased in 1909. It caused annoyance to Whittington and Newbold UDC when used as a snowplough, by sweeping the track clean, but piling the snow on both sides of the roadway!

A splendid picture of that rare bird, Car 15, moving to town off the West Bars loop and spraying everything in sight as it does so. Using a 2,000 gallon tank, this little vehicle could hose a road width of 50ft at a time. After the war it stood neglected, hardly leaving the tramshed. Two cars collided head-on at this loop in December 1918, though without serious casualties.

A superb study of one of the new 16-18 balcony cars supplied by Brush in June 1914, seen here on the traverser. Note the new style lettering and coat-of-arms, and details of the 8ft Peckham Pendulum truck. The electrics have not yet been fitted, and the patent brass bar common to earlier trams has been replaced by a chain.

Balcony double-decker 18 shown off as new on the tramshed loop by Motorman Horace Hall, who appears as a youthful twelve-something in a much earlier plate on page 14. On his right is veteran horse and electric car stalwart Harry Longden. The first two balcony cars made their debut on 11 June 1914, and this shot presumably dates to this time.

Four

Trams and the War (1914-1918)

The first two years of the First World War had little effect on the tramway concern, and early requests for pay increases to offset rising costs received short shrift. The most serious event was the depot fire of 20 October 1916, which was discovered by an inspector at 5.30 a.m., when he found flames pouring from the paint shop. Fifteen cars were in the shed, plus Balcony Car 17, which was undergoing repainting in the shop itself. This tram was completely destroyed, and Car 14 suffered heavy damage to one side. Four other trams were affected by the blaze, but all were repairable, and several others were damaged to a lesser degree. About half the tramshed was destroyed, with part of the roof collapsing backwards into the River Hipper which ran behind the premises. Some of the trams were saved by the staff, who pushed them out of the shed after electric power had been cut off by fire severing the cables.

Car 17 was later totally rebuilt, and Car 14 was revamped with a top-cover and new electrics. Total damage was assessed at £3,000, but unfortunately due to an oversight the 16-18 series trams had never been insured. The insurance company were prepared to make an *ex gratia* payment, but only offered £2,461 against a pared-down Corporation estimate of £2,800.

By late 1916 many of the male staff had been drafted into the armed forces, and female replacements took over the crewing of the rolling stock. A list dated July 1917 shows that thirteen motorwomen and eighteen conductresses were serving with the undertaking. Car spares had become a problem, but the difficulties were alleviated when Sheffield Tramways supplied five sets of magnetic brakes, and Belfast Corporation provided eighteen brand-new traction motors and gear wheels. A minute dated 19 June allowed any tramway employee 'called to the colours' to enjoy his usual week's holiday before joining up, and from the 3 November, just a few days before the Armistice, Sunday working was suspended for reasons of economy.

The Autumn of 1918 was a fraught period as the so-called 'Asian 'flu' pandemic struck Chesterfield with great force, and the natural joy engendered by the end of the war was tempered by the growing death list from this virulent strain of influenza, which hit the transport system badly, and which baffled the medical science of the day. On 14 November only four trams were in service due to the sick list. Amusingly, four days earlier the local factories closed in celebration of Armistice Day, and the 'girl tram drivers' as the local press somewhat disparagingly called them, decided to follow the general example and 'gave the cars a holiday.' Consequently several trams clanked home to base, and the management had to explain to the motorwomen that the facility was still operational!

On 20 November, the longserving Robert Acland gave notice that he was severing his relationship with the town by taking up a post with the Metropolitan Electricity Company at Uxbridge. More than anyone he had been responsible for organizing and guiding the local electricity and tramway undertakings through their formative years, and he would prove hard to replace. Finally, to end the year, there was a violent head-on crash between two trams on West Bars on 16 December, which could have been much worse but for the presence of mind of Motorwoman Millicent Rowbotham, who braked her vehicle hard to lessen the impact between the trams. Casualties were mercifully light among the many passengers due to her action, and she received a suitable award from the Tramways Committee for her actions.

Above: By late 1916 conscription for war service was causing a severe manpower shortage in the Tramways Department. Consequently a number of women were recruited as drivers and conductresses. This lineup, posed in front of one of the fleet vehicles, shows twenty-nine female volunteers. They were trained by male staff such as Chief Inspector Root (centre, middle row), Harry Longden (top right) and Inspector James Bount (centre right).

Left: A fine studio portrait of Conductress No.12, Amy Truman, complete with Bell ticket punch, bag and whistle.

A number of studies of female personnel were taken during the war. Here Elinor, one of the Dowson twins, performs under the eagle eye of the formidable Inspector 'Jimmy' James Blount. The conductress is K. Allen. On her first driving lesson Elinor ran over an unlucky dog, and was all for quitting, till a few well-chosen words from Blount set her straight. The title of the Hippodrome's October effort, with its eternal Shakespearean truth, neatly dates the picture to 1917.

Again featured in this depot shot is the redoubtable Inspector Jimmy Blount appearing on the platform of a balcony car with an unidentified motorwoman. Harry Longden, long-serving horse and electric car veteran, can be seen on the right.

A *rara avis* indeed as scenes including Car 5 are infrequently met with. No.5 shares this regard with two other trams, 3 and 13, both of which are photographically very elusive. The tram betrays evidence of hard usage, and though the motorman is unknown, the conductress is Ellen Burkitt.

George and Agnes Woodhouse, man and wife crew, pose on Car 16 at Brampton terminus. Note the wartime dimmer on the dashlight, and the tethered rope for swinging the trolleyboom. The significance of the sprig of flowers in George's cap is unfortunately unknown!

A wartime studio portrait of George Woodhouse, who began his service as a conductor in 1904. In this study, his cap badge indicates his status as a motorman.

Car 10 at Brampton, with a female display of some fetching straw hats, and Ellen Birkitt in the centre of the group. Chain guards have obviously supplanted the brass bars on the platforms. Patriotic fare adorns the windows, including exhortations to 'Fall In - Answer now in your Country's hour of Need' and 'There's Still a Place in the Line for You! Will You fill it?'

Left: No.11 at Brampton, with more fetching straw headgear, and according to the poster, an ongoing war against the canine species. The well-equipped conductress has not been identified, but Motorman 16 is stalwart Thomas Falconer.

Below: The ticket office and Tramway headquarters at Chatsworth Road, taken in 1917, with Car 17 seen under repair in the tramshed behind. Note the dash panel propped against the wall behind the gate, and the 'Y' junction leading out on to the main thoroughfare.

Above: The tramshed in 1917, showing the 1914 extension on the right for the new balcony cars. Note the pile of controllers on the right, and Car 17 during repainting and refurbishment. This significant photograph was presumably taken after the shed had been rebuilt subsequent to the 1916 fire, and shows the tram undergoing complete reconstruction after that event

Right: This Whittington terminus portrait almost certainly shows a newly completed Tram 17, shown off sometime in late 1917, together with its mixed crew.

A sunny day at Brampton as Motorman Falconer poses on Car 9 with an unknown conductress. The accompanying inspector is James William Cotterill, reputedly not the most popular of the Tramway Department's senior staff, indulging from time to time in fisticuffs with passengers and tram crew. The lack of martial posters suggests a postwar date for this view.

Conductress Elizabeth Kneale, who subsequently married Motorman Charles Hopkinson, is shown in front of one of the 13-14 class cars, though the truck details differ from the one shown under the Shopping Week car of 1910, suggesting that this conveyance may have been re-trucked at a later date. The axlebox is certainly not of the Brush Flexible Axle type.

An all-female crew smile for the camera as Motorwoman Millicent Rowbotham, accompanied by Elizabeth Kneale, takes the controls of Car 18 in this late 1918 photograph. In December of that year Millicent was involved in a head-on tram smash on West Bars, but lessened the severity of the collision by braking her car to a swift stop to lessen the impact. Her cool-headedness undoubtedly prevented a more serious accident, and the Tramways Committee awarded her £1 for her devotion to duty.

Chesterfield Corporation Tramways

FARES

TO OR FROM

Brampton and Gas Works	1d.
Walton Road and Stephenson Place	1d.
Gas Works and Albert Street	1d.
Stephenson Place and Dark Lane	1d.
Albert Street and Whittington	1d.
Brampton and Stephenson Place	1½d.
Brampton and Market Place	1½d.
Stephenson Place and Whittington	1½d.
Gas Works and Dark Lane	1½d.
Walton Road and Dark Lane	2d.
Brampton and Albert Street	2½d.
Gas Works and Whittington	2½d.
Through	3d.

WORKMEN'S CARS

Before 8 a.m. from Brampton or Whittington and 8-10 a.m. from Market Place.

Brampton and Stephenson Place	1d.
Stephenson Place and Whittington	1d.
Walton Road and Albert Street	1d.

Children over 3 Years of Age must be paid for.

Children under the age of 10 are allowed to travel for a 1d. over a 1½d. Section.

No fares or excess fares less than One Penny will be accepted.

No Through Tickets between Brampton and Whittington will be issued unless a Through Service is run.

No change can be given by the Conductor for a coin of larger value than Half-a-Crown.

PASSENGERS ARE RESPECTFULLY REQUESTED TO OBSERVE THAT THE CONDUCTOR PUNCHES A TICKET REPRESENTING THE VALUE OF THE FARE PAID FOR AND THE SECTION TO BE TRAVELLED OVER.

PASSENGERS MUST NOT GET ON OR LEAVE THE CAR WHILE IN MOTION.

TRAMWAY DEPOT,
    172, CHATSWORTH ROAD,
APRIL, 1919.

R. L. ACLAND, M.Inst.E.E.,
    Engineer.

April 1919 saw the first act in an ongoing hike of tramway fares. There were further doses of the same medicine in December 1919, November 1920 and April 1922. As a result the cost of a through journey rose from 3d to 8d, signalling passenger rates that were among the highest in the country.

Five

The Tramway Post-War (1918-1927)

By 1919 the Chesterfield track, trams and overhead were all in dire need of refurbishment, and in that year six open-top cars – 6, 7, 8, 11 and 12 – were modernized by being given top-covers. Around the same time all the trams were divested of their clumsy indicator boxes, which were replaced with oyster lamps. The running wire was renewed by British Helsby at a cost of £1,379, and in 1920-1921, £13,000 was expended on the track, in order to extend its life by some five years. In the latter year the female staff were summarily dismissed and by December the crews were again all-male. One car was fitted with a screen at one end as an experiment, but no other trams were converted, and drivers remained open to the elements to the end. In 1923 the Market Place spur was abandoned to construct underground toilets, and a new stopping place was fixed in New Square.

The new manager Robert Campion was instructed to study trolleybus systems, as moves were afoot to replace the ageing and expensive to ride trams with railless vehicles. By 1924 the track was giving further cause for concern, and was patched up to prolong its survival. A paper by Alfred Baker, of Birmingham Tramways, who was commissioned to report on the facility, recommended the substitution of trolleybuses for trams, which could use Corporation electricity and existing traction poles, but the council vote between trackless cars and motorbuses was close, despite a second report on the system by new manager George Margrave, who also supported the trolleybus lobby. Margrave was replaced as manager by Walter Marks in 1925, and he was eventually directed to convert the undertaking to railless running, which was agreed that same year after some fierce in-fighting in several council and committee battles.

By 1925 both track and trams were decrepit, with the latter suffering severely from the worn-out rails. In April 1926 trolleybuses were given the go-ahead, and Clough-Smith was awarded the contract to supply fourteen single-deck vehicles at a cost of £1,859 each. The overhead was to be converted at a cost of £23,947, and repairs to trams and tramline were cut to an absolute minimum 'having in mind the discontinuance of the service.' In February 1927 work on the Brampton wiring was commenced, and the trams were switched to the town-Whittington run, motorbuses taking over the Brampton route from the former. All the open-top cars were retired at this time, and the Whittington route was serviced by the surviving top-covered vehicles.

23 May 1927 was the date scheduled for tramway abandonment, and on a cool, rainy evening, Car 14, rather tattily bedecked with flags and bunting, carried Corporation dignitaries and guests on a final ride from Stephenson Place to Whittington, cheered on by the

considerable crowds who lined the whole route. At Whittington Moor a huge throng gave the old veteran, driven by Harry Longden, a resounding welcome, as the committee disembarked for the regulation photographs. On the return trip the car lurched to a stop at Pottery Lane, as a seven-inch piece of broken track jammed itself beneath the wheels. After the tram had safely negotiated the obstruction, the offending length of metal was presented to Chairman Robinson!

At the depot another crowd awaited the old war-horse which pulled up on the loop for the obligatory 'old and new' shot, the tram posing alongside one of the spanking new trolleybuses. Car 14 then disappeared into the tramshed and oblivion, as Straker 1, loaded up with the *prominenti*, whined off in the direction of town. Immediately afterwards the first five trackless vehicles commenced the inauguration of the new service, leaving the hardworking trams to disappear into oblivion. During their busy lifetime they had run no less than 6,245,426 miles, and had freighted 73,222,529 passengers.

Balcony car 17 pictured at Brampton with its post-war all-male crew. The indicator boxes have disappeared, and the advertisements are more discreet than in earlier views.

A singular shot, showing as it does Car 14, seriously damaged in the depot fire of 1916, after its rebuild, which included the top-cover seen here. The electrics were also upgraded, with T1 controllers replacing the smaller 90Ms. The conductor is Tommy Baker.

74

A fine study of Car 12 at Brampton in 1920 after the fitting of a top-cover. Note the new coat-of-arms, and the non-standard diminutive lettering on the rocker panel. The motorman is Jack Gretton, the conductress Elizabeth Kneale.

Car 6, also shown at Brampton post-war, again with top-cover, and bearing a distinctly worse-for-wear appearance, with sagging platforms and weathered upperworks. On this tram the neat early gold lettering has been replaced by larger black characters. The motorman is Jack Rouse, the conductor Gary Gascoyne.

Tramcar 4 at Brampton, in a picturesque setting and deplorable looking condition. The mixed crew hints at an early 1920s date, as the remaining female employees were eased out of their jobs by the end of 1921, to make way for men. Car 4 was phased out of service in October 1925, after an accident. Note that oyster lamps have replaced the destination boxes.

On 7 August 1922, flash floods inundated Chatsworth Road as the River Hipper overflowed. Here one of the balcony cars is stranded below Barker Lane, with the Congregational Church on the left, as the rising waters brought the system to a standstill.

Car 8 paid an unscheduled call on Watson's Butchers at Stonegravels at 7 p.m. on 18 October 1926. The tram, driven by Thomas Falconer, broke an axle and jumped the points at the Albert Street loop. Mercifully the traction pole prevented it from toppling and causing a more serious mishap. Amazingly only three riders were injured, plus the driver, who suffered a broken ankle, and a boy in the shop, cut by flying glass. The car was back on the road in early December. Note the destination boards in the window, the metal stop sign on the pole, and the black lettering on the rocker panel.

A 1920s vista of Stephenson Place, showing the sharp curve of the twin track leading to the facing crossover where open-top Car 10 awaits traffic on the left-hand track, which was used as a weekend terminus. The façade of Deacon's Bank, built in 1906, dominates the junction, and a back-seat lady driver directs operations in the imposing automobile on the right.

Opposite top: New Square in 1923, with Car 16 pausing by the Portland Hotel on its way to Brampton from the Low Pavement spur off to the left. In the foreground the single line opens out into double track, and the wear and tear on the points at this spot, with trams rattling over them every few minutes, can well be imagined.

Compare the previous picture with this one, which was taken in May 1927, as the conductor swings the trolleypole of Car 7, waiting at the terminus in preparation for the journey to Whittington. The Brampton section had been converted for trolleybus operation by this time and the aggressive-looking Bristol motorbus No.30 (RA 441) on the right was providing a temporary service along this route.

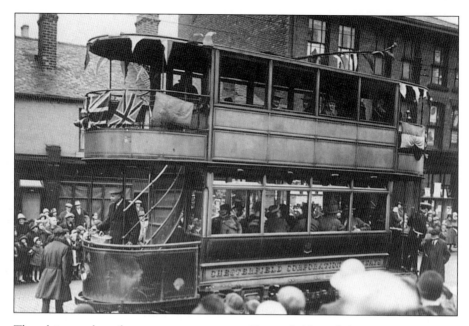

The ultimate day of tramway operation in Chesterfield, and doesn't it show! The demise of the tram is aptly summed up in this shot, as Car 14, dented, dilapidated and in need of a good wash, arrives on its final run to Whittington on 23 May 1927, bearing the usual dignitaries. The driver is Harry Longden, by now night foreman at the tram depot.

The Tramways Committee line up in a variety of natty headgear in front of Car 14, bunting whipped by a stiff breeze. The members include Philip Robinson, the tall central figure, with Harry Cropper on his right, and Ernest Shentall, with umbrella, to his left. Walter Marks is extreme right, with Harry Longden behind.

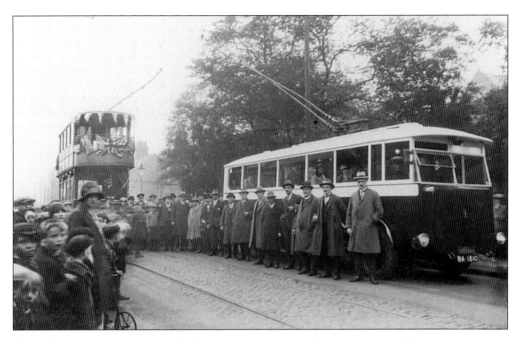

The old meets the new outside the tram depot later the same day as Car 14 poses by its replacement, Straker Clough No.1 (RA 1810), resplendent in its livery of Suffield green and white. The driver of the trolleybus is Bill Hardwick, and from right to left the posed lineup includes Philip Robinson, Harry Cropper, and fourth from right, Walter Marks.

The surging crowds take a last look at the depot, following the terminal ride of Car 14, seen on the left. Tram 7 inevitably also gets in on the act. All the cars seem to have discarded their advertising in the last period of service.

Members of the Corporation Trackless Sub-Committee seen on a trial run at Brampton terminus in front of Straker 1 (RA 1810). This group, led by Philip Robinson, pushed through the trolleybus replacement of the tram in the teeth of opposition both in council and in the local press.

Six

The Restoration of Chesterfield Car 7 (1993-1996)

Brush Electric Car 7 was one of the earliest of the twelve trams ordered to reach Chesterfield. It participated in the early trials along the Brampton part of the system, and throughout its life it was a particular favourite with the camera; there are far more shots of it in service than any other fleet vehicle. The tram was damaged in the depot fire of 1916, and it was subsequently top-covered and had its electrics updated, with new T1 controllers. During the final two years of tramcar operation it covered 48,328 miles, and was running on the final afternoon of 23 May 1927, when it clocked up eighty-five miles on its swansong.

All the car bodies were put up for sale, and No.7 was purchased by local builder Sam Wheatcroft, who sold it on to John Cocking who had it transported to Two Dales. There both decks were set up side-by-side in a field perched on a brick foundation and joined by a connecting corridor. Divided into living quarters and bedrooms, with the lower saloon enclosed and fitted with end windows, the structure served first as a holiday home, sleeping eight people, and later as a rather basic residence for a family relative, Florrie Sharpe. After her death the Tramway Museum Society (TMS) purchased the derelict property from the Mappin family from whom the Cockings had leased the land on which the tram bodies had rested. Both tram saloons were subsequently removed into storage at Clay Cross in 1973, where they languished for many years. In 1991 the Tramcar Sponsorship Organization (TSO) informed the TMS that their members had voted to rebuild Chesterfield 7 in post First World War guise with their funding, plus a Science Museum grant, despite the fact that the vehicle languished in the lowest category of proposed future projects, and full-time work commenced two years later.

The chosen truck was a Peckham P22, as no Brush Radials had survived the sixty-odd years since Car 7 had last run. The tram was gradually reconstructed using original materials, parts from other cars salvaged in the Chesterfield locality and elsewhere, and other components built up from scratch. The conveyance boasted Westinghouse T2 controllers, and the patent brass bar and folding step arrangement originally installed by the Brush Company. The upper saloon was lowered into position on 14 December 1995, the two halves united together for the first time in nearly seventy years. By September 1996 the car was completed, in its Carmine and Primrose livery, with the appropriate lettering and lining-out, and was ready for initial trials. On 7 November the vehicle was first tested on the Crich rails; problems with the electrics were gradually sorted out, including an initial tendency to move in reverse!

Travelling under the power of its 40hp BTH motors, much more lively than its original 25hp

Westinghouse 90Ms, the tram had its brakes tested, and its first passenger run took place on 22 December 1996. The inaugural public display, with the appropriate ceremony, took place at Crich Tramway Museum on Saturday 7 May (one week short of the seventieth anniversary of tramway abandonment in Chesterfield), in front of enthusiastic crowds, and the car entered service later that same day. The whole restoration consumed three years, involved 14,000 man hours, and cost over £120,000. This splendid tramcar, lovingly and caringly renovated by John Shawcross and his Crich team, will give many years' service at the museum, and stands as a testament to the work of the TMS and the TSO.

When the trams were abandoned, Mr John Cocking transported Car 7 to Two Dales, where it did duty over many years as a holiday home. In this post-war view, the owner struggles with his Austin 7, with the side-by-side saloons of the tram behind him, connected by a covered corridor.

The fairly dilapidated lower saloon on display at Clay Cross in 1989. In 1991 the Tramcar Sponsorship Organization offered to fund the restoration of Car 7 under their *aegis*. The project went ahead in 1993.

The upper deck, in equally disreputable condition, likewise languishes at Clay Cross in 1989, behind its long-separated partner.

The weathered components of the lower saloon are here displayed in the workshop at Crich, at an early stage of the rebuilding in January 1994.

The upper saloon of Car 7 is shown here under construction in November 1995, with the completed and painted trucked lower deck just visible behind.

14 December 1996, and the upper saloon is just about to be reunited with its partner after some seventy years apart.

Skilful work with the crane ensures that the two component parts of Car 7 are coupled together again to form a complete tramcar.

The bodies of Chesterfield Electric Car 7 are connected together again, an historic moment in the resurrection of the tram. The details of the Peckham truck show up clearly in this photograph.

In immaculate state after its refurbishment, No.7 is shown here on its early trials in October 1996, with its patent brass platform bar and step in the folded position. Great credit is due to the workshop staff for their loving and careful restoration.

Motorman Peter Biggs eases Car 7 out of Shed 3 at Crich on a misty morning on Saturday 17 May 1997. The occasion was the celebratory inaugural run of this latest of Crich's successful rebuilds.

The author tries his hand at piloting an unblemished Car 7 at Crich on 11 October 1999, by kind permission of John Shawcross and the Tramway Museum staff.

Mr Squire Sellars, who owned the High Street drapery pictured behind
Car 6, hired and decorated the vehicle for the opening day run on 7
August 1903. Motorman John William Phair stands alongside the tram,
while Mr Sellars' senior staff occupy the top deck.

Seven

Glossop Tramways (1903-1927)

The Glossop Tramway was the second electric tramway constructed in Derbyshire, and was a surprising choice for such a facility, located as it was in a small and isolated mill town with a static population. Perhaps it was hoped that the enterprise would transport the large numbers of cotton mill workers who held jobs at the many factories along the route at a cheap rate. A further attraction was the possibility of a connection with the vast Stalybridge, Hyde, Mossley and Dukinfield Joint Board network, (SHMD), whose lines, covering the eastern side of Manchester, ran as close as Mottram, a scant two miles from Woolley Bridge on the county border.

The line was the product of local enterprise, suggested by Glossop-born Charles Knowles, who worked for the Urban Electricity Supply Company (UESC). He was duly appointed engineer and manager of the enterprise. In November 1900 the company promulgated a provisional order to provide a tramway and an electricity supply to the town, as they also did for Camborne and Redruth in Cornwall, their only other tramway. The track was planned as an inverted 'C', four miles long, running central to the road, with the north-west terminus at Hadfield, and the south-east at Old Glossop, joining relatively undeveloped stretches of roadway which was studded with factories and large mills. A half-mile spur, known as the Whitfield branch, ran south off the main track to Charlestown.

The route was laid as single track with turnouts, with ten loops on the main route and one on the spur, at a gauge of 4ft 8½in, the same as that of the Manchester undertaking. A site at Dinting, on the north bank of the Glossop Brook, was selected for the tram depot and power station, and by December 1902, after some heel-dragging, the tracklaying was well under way. The running wire was carried for the most part on bracket poles which were completely functional, with no ornamental scrollwork whatever. Seven open-top double-deck cars were ordered from G.F. Milnes of Hadley, all fitted with the hard-riding 6ft wheelbase German girder trucks then in use by the firm. They featured reversed staircases, had a forty-eight seat capacity, and were painted in dark green and primrose, with plain lining-out, and the legend GLOSSOP TRAMWAYS in gold on the rocker panels.

The power station was ready for operation in August 1903, and the first tram trial took place on the 7th of that month. With all seven vehicles ready for service, the formal opening was fixed for the 20th, but the Board of Trade inspection of the line had to be deferred until the 21st. The opening went ahead as scheduled, with the cars decorated with flags and bunting, but services were deferred for a further day. The chosen guests retired for lunch and laudatory speeches to the success of the enterprise, and a local draper, Mr Squire Sellars, hired a tram and filled it with his relations and staff for the occasion.

Service cars commenced running on the 21st, and as with most facilities, the early years were fruitful, despite initial problems with timetables and passing places. By January 1904 the enterprise had freighted its first half million riders, though the Whitfield branch proved something of a white elephant. It 'practically ran empty' and in August an enclosed single-deck one-man demi-car, No.8 in the fleet, built by the British Electric Car Company of Trafford Park, and capable of carrying twenty-two passengers, arrived to take over operations on the spur. It must have been a popular vehicle to man in winter, with its full driver protection, as opposed to the open platforms of the Milnes trams, though it was rarely filled to capacity.

The line never went into profit, which was hardly surprising as the population served was only 22,000. Weekly receipts hovered around the £100 mark, and there was a failure, despite several attempts, to secure a connection with the vast Manchester networks to the west. The most promising plans for a linkup with the SHMD were killed off by the First World War, after gaining Royal Assent in 1915. The overhead and traction poles tended to suffer from the effects of 'the corrosive nature of the Glossop atmosphere', doubtless fuelled by the smoke and grime from the many local industries, and there was a heavy Company outlay on repairs to the track. However by 1912, times became more prosperous and Knowles began seeking to augment the rolling stock. Nevertheless, it was not until 1918 that he was able to purchase an ex-Sheffield single-deck tram, mounted on a 7ft Brill 21E truck, and extensively overhauled, with transverse seating for twenty-eight passengers, and drop windows. Costing £350, the Electric Railway and Tramway Carriage Works, Preston, constructed tramcar went into service in March 1918 as Glossop 9, but it is a moot point as to whether it ever received the Company colours, or if it ran in the Sheffield livery of dark blue and cream.

By the early 1920s the line was in deep difficulty, its problems exacerbated not only by wartime shortages and rising costs, but by friction between the Glossop public and the UESC. The former felt that the undertaking was being run simply for company profit, with little regard to the travelling population, and with rising journey prices and timetable alterations that were not always justified. The Whitfield spur was closed in the autumn of 1918 as a fuel saving measure, and was never re-opened, despite the Town Council's demand that it should be. The tram crews too were disgruntled, as cuts were made to their working hours, and their wages failed to reflect rising costs of living. In fact, with track and trams deteriorating, the UESC attempted to sell the facility to the Town Council, but the latter sensibly refused to place the millstone around their own collective necks.

In June 1920 the car crews went on a ten-day strike in an effort to improve their basic wages. The action was a complete failure, and the men were forced back to work on the company's terms. By 1923 the Joint Board had obtained an act to allow motorbuses to ply the tramway route under the terms of the 1915 agreement, providing unwelcome competition. The trams continued to operate, the ride doubtless becoming bumpier, though the facility still carried around a million travellers and managed around 180,000 route miles per year, though the percentage of working costs to passenger receipts steadily worsened. In November 1927 the UESC again offered the system to Glossop Council, indicating they were willing to transfer the cars into municipal ownership if the latter were willing to use the Company power supply. The offer was refused, and the Company announced its intention of closing down the tramway on Christmas Eve.

The last cars left both termini at 11 p.m. that night, rattling their way into oblivion. Thirty employees received severance pay of £5 – a fine Christmas present! – and were then out of work. On Boxing Day the North Western Company opened an omnibus service along the abandoned route. In April 1928 the UESC began removing the rails and reinstating the roadway. A twenty-four year episode was finally closed, and one might comment, following Shakespeare's unlucky *King Lear* 'The wonder is it hath endured so long.'

Nineteen tram crew pose in smart new 'maternity jacket' rig in front of one of the new cars at the Dinting tramshed. Superintendent Emmot takes the controls, flanked on his right by Charles Knowles, the General Manager. The majority of staff display fashionable hirsute adornment, while the superintendent sports a full set!

Another shot of eighteen tram staff showing off another rig, perhaps an alternative summer uniform. Two inspectors flank the nattily dressed and unidentified gentleman in the centre front of the photograph.

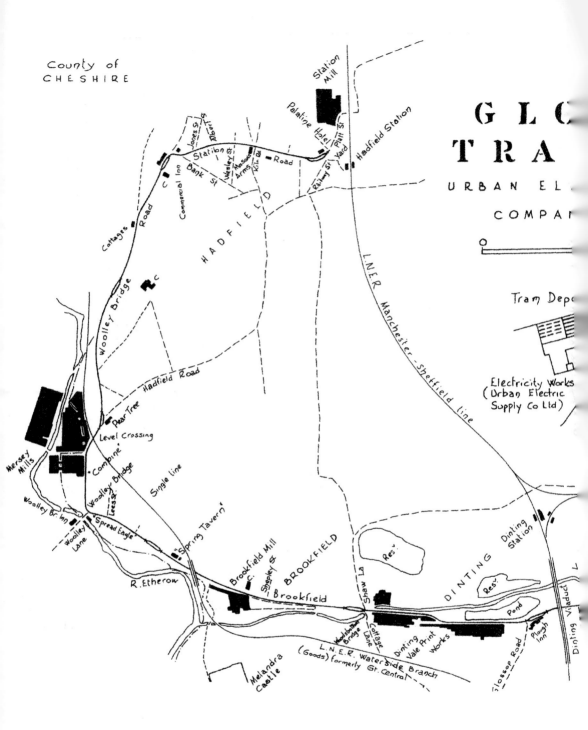

The Glossop track layout formed an inverted 'C' four miles long, though the termini at Hadfield and Old Glossop were only some 1½ miles apart as the crow flies. Note the Whitfield spur at the bottom right hand of the plan.

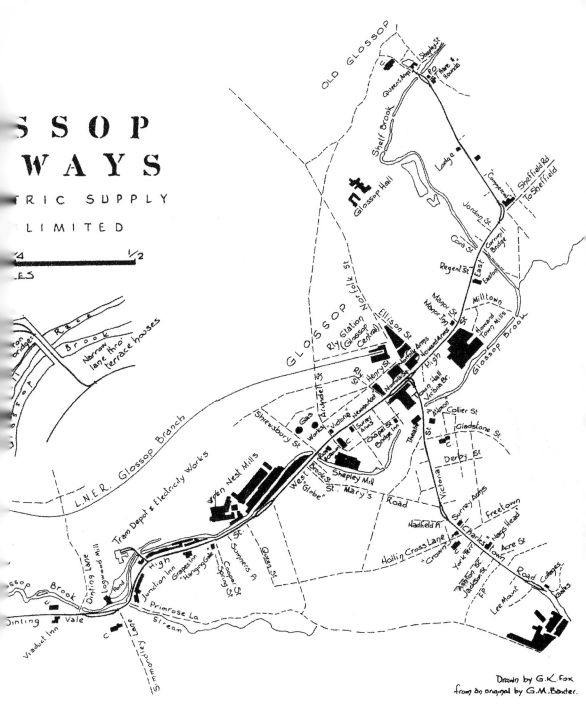

SSOP
WAYS
TRIC SUPPLY
LIMITED

Drawn by G.K.Fox
from an original by G.M.Baxter.

An excellent postcard view of one of the brand-new cars, picking out the livery, truck details and lettering. Note the track brake in position, and the early luxury of lower saloon curtaining.

A service car waits outside the Palatine and Railway Hotel, opposite the railway station at the Hadfield terminus. Tram and crew pose on the loop, with Station Road on the left.

A vista taken at the Hadfield terminus near the end of tramway service, with a rival North Western omnibus awaiting custom with one wheel on the turnout. The building on the left is the library.

Well-laden Car 3 is shown at the Old Glossop terminus on 21 August 1903, with no less than three taverns within close drinking distance of the stop. The landlord posed at the door of the Queen's Arms doubtless contemplates increased profits as thirsty riders disembark. The tram conductor evidently rejoiced in the name of 'Masher' Howard.

Car 1 climbs the cobbled thoroughfare of Station Road towards Hadfield terminus, passing Salisbury Street on the left. Note the plain and unadorned traction poles, and the offset trolleypole on the tram, which has HADFIELD painted round the dashlamp. The usual bystanders add animation to the scene.

Car 3, well freighted with young ladies perhaps on an outing, descends Station Road near Lambgates in the early years of the service. The board hung on the dash panel indicates the vehicle serves both the main line and the Whitfield spur.

A fully-patronized and worse-for-wear Car 3 conveying its cargo of cloth-capped mill workers on a short working to Woolley Bridge. The tram is progressing along Woolley Bridge Road, near the junction with Bank Bottom.

The spectacular Dinting Viaduct dominates the scene as the line passes through the open Dinting Vale. Car 7 heads north-west, the dash panel notice indicating that it serves both Old Glossop and the spur line. Holy Trinity Church is on the right, and beyond the arch on the left is the Plough Inn, the halfway stage on the main route.

This junction, where Primrose Lane and Dinting Vale meet High Street West, shows the single line of the tramway, and, on the left, the UESC power station with the tramshed to the rear.

The unimposing central gap between the terraces on High Street West, behind the photographer's youthful audience, was the entrance to the tram depot, reached via a bridge over the Glossop Brook. Swann's fine clock shows the time as 12.16 p.m. and one can sympathize with the householders on both sides of the opening, as cars clanked onto the main road in the early hours of the morning!

An excellent tramscape of High Street West, from a postcard franked August 1905, with Arundel Street on the left, and Car 5 moving towards Hadfield. Note the advert on the dash, and the young man-about-town, posing on the left-hand pavement with double watch chain on display.

An unidentified car waits on the Norfolk Square loop, with the Town Hall looming on the right. This card was produced for Boot's Cash Chemists, whose shop is on the extreme right, incidentally boasting a fine window display.

The Town Hall again, topped by an elaborate clock tower, and a service tram waiting on the turnout for trade to Old Glossop. The tall chimney and upperworks of Howard Town Mills loom up on the left.

An interesting view taken around Wakes Week in 1923, and clearly showing the twin track curving right into Victoria Street, and the Whitfield spur. The running wire for the line is still *in situ*, though the service ceased operation in 1918. The main line continues along High Street East.

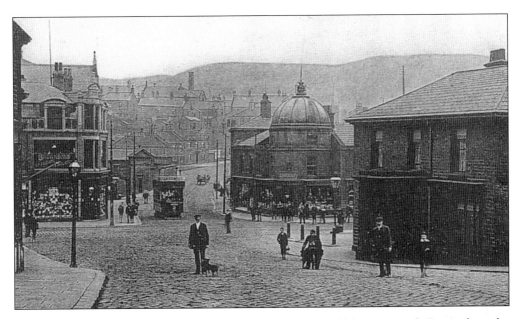

This prospect, looking down Norfolk Street, reveals a sea of cobblestones, with Car 1 taking the Whitfield line by the prominent dome of Bradbury's Corner. The background to this shot has been heavily retouched.

A car moves down Victoria Street in the first year or two of the system, heading along the spur towards town, with the rustic-looking theatre on the right, and the Albion Hotel visible behind the tram.

A close-up from a Victoria Street scene showing a pre-First World War Church Walk, but revealing other noteworthy details. The little demi-car is caught among the worshippers in their Sunday best, and immediately behind it an open-top tram moves along High Street with two ladies occupying the upper deck front seats. The left-hand tram standard bears a stop sign.

The east end of High Street East discloses rows of well-built terraces along the line of the tramway. In the distance the Commercial Hotel can just be glimpsed as the tramtracks swing hard left on to Hall Street and the final stretch of the main line. In the foreground four proud ladies display bouncing babies for the benefit of the camera.

The meeting of High Street East and Hall Street (renamed Manor Park Road in 1926) had a loop laid in the bend, which Car 6 is just entering. The Commercial Hotel stands on the right, and on the left a splendid water trough supports some fine ornamental ironwork and a street lamp. A feeder box stands alongside the left hand bracket pole.

Children play happily at the same junction, as the empty-looking service car passes the water fountain on the $2\frac{1}{2}$ minute journey to the town centre. Note the total lack of other traffic in both photographs.

The Old Glossop terminus, showing two of the three public houses nearby, the Talbot Inn, with the Hare and Hounds beyond. The line here terminated in a loop, with a short length of single track beyond, in front of the horse's hoofs.

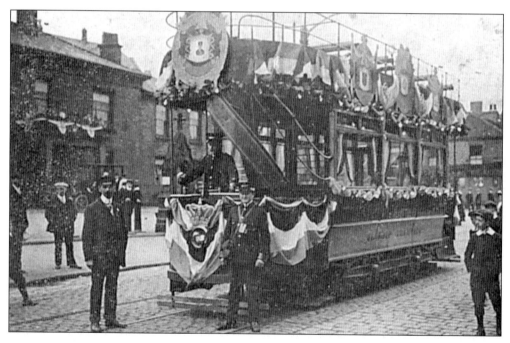

A decorated tramcar pictured in Norfolk Square, with Superintendent Emmot on the left. Although the date and occasion are unknown, the bells, portraits and garlands suggest it celebrated a wedding, perhaps involving one of the tramway staff.

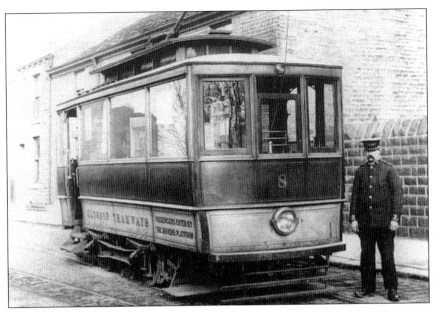

A superb study of Demi-Car 8 at the Charlestown Road terminus, outside the gates of Whitfield House, now the entrance to Glossop Fire Station. Motorman John Byrom stands alongside his charge, in appropriate heavy-duty footwear. A pre-service shot of this little tram taken in 1904 suggests it may have been re-trucked at some time in its life.

In 1918 the tramway took delivery of a single-deck ex-Sheffield car, No.56, seen here in earlier service in the city. The 'SV' sign indicated its usual route as Spring Vale. The UESC probably ran the tram in its Sheffield livery.

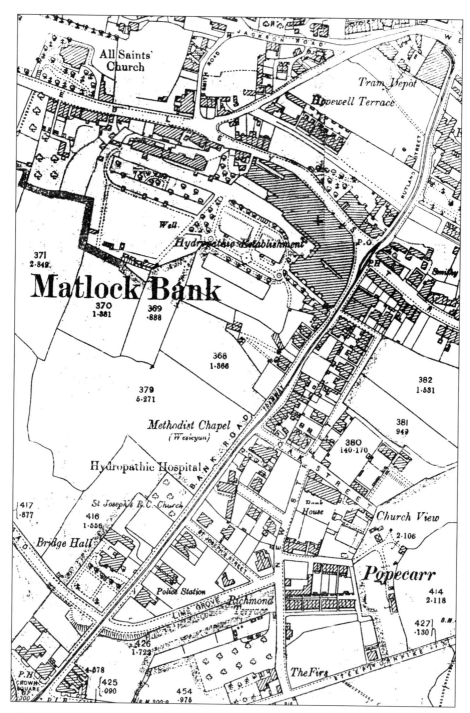

The cable tramway ran for over half a mile up the steep one-in-five incline. The plan shows the track layout, with loops in Crown Square (bottom left) and at Smedley Street to the right of Smedley's Hydro. The tramshed was at the top of the hill (top right) alongside the generating station.

Eight
The Matlock Cable Tramway (1893-1927)

The Matlock Cable Tramway has a number of claims to fame, the first being that it was the earliest non-horse tramway to be constructed in the county. Its origins can be traced to the period when the small town was chosen by John Smedley as the site for a hydro in 1853. Hydropathic establishments were springing up rapidly in numerous spa towns at this time, and Smedley's undertaking on the steep Matlock Bank was followed by a number of competitors who set up in business on the same hillside. Matlock entered a boom period as votaries flocked to punish themselves in the name of health, and with the new customers came shops to cater for them. This period of expansion was helped by the arrival of the railway linking Matlock with London and Manchester, and the town swiftly attained the status of a widely patronized inland resort.

The idea for a tramway linking Crown Square at the foot of the hill with the top of Matlock Bank originated with Job Smith, a native of the town, who in 1862 first saw the new cable trams in San Fransisco. He suggested to Smedley that a similar system up Matlock hill might prove a sound investment, linking the railway with the hillside spas. The idea languished for some years, but on his return Smith had his proposed route surveyed. However the highest part of the suggested line, Rutland Street, was too narrow for trams, and the project once more lapsed. Smith mooted the project again in 1890, and as a new member of the local board was able to give it a more thorough airing, especially as the offending street had been widened. G. Croydon Marks, engineer to the Lynton Cliff Railway, saw a report on the scheme, and discussed it with George Newnes MP, a noted publisher whose periodicals included that respected organ of public opinion *Tit Bits*, and who was a Matlock native. Newnes offered to finance the undertaking, and a company was formed for this purpose. After powers had been granted, work commenced on the depot. A suggestion to erect it near Matlock Bridge was rejected as the River Derwent periodically overflowed in that area; consequently the building was shifted uphill to the corner of Rutland and Wellington Streets. Marks became the company engineer, and called in William Colam, a specialist in cable traction, as adviser.

The contract for laying the line was let to Dick, Kerr & Co., who began work in March 1892. It was designed as a single track, 0.62 miles long, with a passing loop at Smedley Street, halfway up the slope. Two further records now fell to the infant line; it became the first single-line cable tramway in Europe, and the maximum gradient – 1ft in $5\frac{1}{2}$ – made it the steepest street tramway anywhere in the world. The track gauge was fixed at 3ft 6in with a central slot rail beneath which ran a conduit holding the continuous 3in cable. This ran endlessly in its channel from the steam-powered engine room, round a tensioning mechanism and guiding rails, down the hill, round further wheels in an underground chamber in Crown Square and back up the hill again. The route contained some sharp curves, one of 40ft radius, which necessitated special pulleys to support and carry the cable round. The track climbed an elevation of 300ft in 2,300 to the upper terminus alongside the depot.

The trial trip on 12 November 1892 was run at a speed of 6mph, with G.F. Milnes of Hadley supplying the three cars, all open-top double-deckers with transverse garden seats with reversible backs on both decks, providing thirteen inside places, and eighteen outside. They were painted in royal blue and white, with numbers on both dash panels, and the company logo on the waist. They were mounted on equal four-wheel bogies and had two braking systems, one an emergency one to the rail, powerful enough to stop the vehicle when free-running. To start the car the driver operated a 'gripper' mounted under the staircase at each end of the tram body. This undercar device passed through the narrow slot in the rail, and had a clamp or vice at its base. By turning a screw via a handwheel the driver could lock the soft metal jaws of the gripper to the continuously moving cable. To stop the tram he released the cable by opening the jaws, and applying the brake. Both brakes were workable from either platform, by the driver or conductor.

The completed tramway was inspected on 7 March 1893 by Major General Hutchinson, who warmly praised the efficiency of the brakes, and fixed the cable speed at $5\frac{1}{2}$ mph. There was a loop in Crown Square, and at the depot a sharp left turn brought the cars into a yard where the vehicles could stand on the level. A depot traverser led to three short tracks, each holding one tram. The service was normally run by two vehicles, which counterbalanced each other, with a third on standby. There were problems with the last car uphill at night, always heavily laden, which struggled up the bank at a snail's pace! The depot, which boasted a 100ft tall chimney together with a waiting room, and 'other conveniences', cost £2,600.

The line opened on 28 March 1893 with great pomp and ceremony, and an inaugural booklet was published to commemorate the event. The whole town was en fête for the occasion, with flags and banners everywhere, the routeway decorated with floral arches, streamers, and further flags. The procession boasted a host of local dignitaries who proceeded to the depot, where the engines were started and the return journey made by tramcar. A banquet at the Assembly Rooms was attended by 120 guests, and was followed by a series of laudatory speeches heralding the newly installed facility, which joined the elite few cable tramways operating in Britain.

During the opening year the newfangled system was a great success, transporting 252,633 passengers during the high season. There was a profit of £204, and a 2% dividend was declared on the £15,000 share capital. Sadly, this was the only dividend ever enjoyed by the shareholders. Cables only lasted on average two years, probably due to the wear caused by the short radius curves. After five years of operation, Newnes, by now a knight, bought out his fellow shareholders and presented the undertaking as a gift to the town. On 28 June 1898 it was handed over to Matlock UDC, a formal ceremony following on 26 October. The council thus became the first municipal authority to own a cable tramway, and the only one to acquire one as a gift! By this time it was realized that the system was more an amenity than a profit-making concern, though for a number of years losses were only modest.

In 1899 a picturesque tram shelter was built in Crown Square, surmounted by a fine public clock with four faces and topped by ornamental iron scrollwork, both donated by Robert Wildgoose. The ornate little edifice appears in many photographs taken during the tramway period, and afterwards was removed and rebuilt in a nearby park. When the council took over the cable cars the legend MATLOCK URBAN DISTRICT COUNCIL TRAMWAY appeared on the cant rail above the tram windows. Gradually advertising material was added to the conveyances, many of them related to the plethora of hydropathic establishments which flourished along the Bank.

After municipalization the trams continued their valuable service up the hill, and in 1911 a fourth vehicle, a locally-built single-decker, adapted from a double-decked Birmingham cable car, was added to the fleet to provide a four-car running schedule for passengers. Unfortunately the tram was provided with longitudinal seating, and riders found themselves sliding to the bottom end of the conveyance as it moved up and down the track. The car was dispensed with during the First World War, being sold off in 1916. To enhance the image of the resort, the crews were equipped with new uniforms every Good Friday, the official start of the holiday season, and the smart turn-out doubtless created a favourable impression on the early visitors. As time passed it became increasingly apparent that the system was not a financial success, though up to 1913 losses were acceptable, perhaps £800 over the preceding twenty years. A modest profit of £17 was achieved in 1910, when fares were 2*d* up the hill, and a penny down. From 1917 the financial position deteriorated rapidly, and the UDC faced deficits of around £1,000 a year, one of the problems being increasing maintenance costs. In 1920 the expensive steam engines were replaced by a gas plant, but winter month losses that year totalled £955. Fares were uprated, but losses continued to mount, and a rival motorbus service, touching both termini via a circuitous route, put further pressure on the ailing cableway.

In July 1927 there were proposals in council to end the service, one member reckoning that it had suffered losses of between £30,000 and £50,000 since 1898. The hotly-disputed issue was put to a public vote, and the result was for dispensing with the tramway. A council meeting on 5 September ratified a previous UDC decision to scrap the cars on the 30th by a two-thirds majority, but before that date the system literally came to a sudden stop as the cable broke. At its final demise the undertaking added a last record to its laurels as the final cable tramway to operate on the British mainland. The tram bodies were duly sold off at £5 each, while the cable, rails and gas engine realized £250. Though its passing was predictable in the climate of the time, one can only speculate what a tourist feature the tramway would be in this present age, bearing in mind the modern attractions available in nearby Matlock Bath.

The tram depot, built at a cost of £2,600, boasted a 100ft tall chimney, plus offices and a waiting room. The double doors of the carshed can be seen on the right of the photograph.

This shot, taken in Crown Square in 1892, shows the loop, and the central slot in the rail to take the tram gripper. Job Smith can be seen fourth from the left in one of the fancy western-style hats he affected.

Laying the rail on the steepest part of the Bank, on Rutland Street. The gritstone setts piled alongside the track were used as paving to cover all but the tramlines. Note the sharp curve to the line in the distance.

Job Smith was the driving force behind
the inauguration of the cable tramline.
He owned Malvern House Hydro on
Smedley Street, and was a councillor for
the Matlock UDC, which enabled him
to apply pressure in favour of the project.

G. Croydon Marks had extensive
experience in steep-gradient
tramway work, and was appointed
by George Newnes as engineer to
the Matlock cable tram project.

An excellent view of Car 3 on the turnout at Smedley Street at the inauguration of the service, picking out its salient features. Note the triangular dash panel, with the entrance step on the left. The ever-present Job Smith can be seen halfway along the well-patronized upper deck. The Tramway Engineer, G.C. Marks, appears on the extreme right of the vehicle.

The spartan interior of the cars can be appreciated in this view, which shows off the turtle-back roof, and the two-and-one arrangement of the wooden seats. Advertising is even carried on the side of the ceiling, proclaiming George Statham's Dining Rooms. He was probably related to the photographer, W.N. Statham.

The Crown Square tram terminus as seen from Matlock Bridge and the approach via the railway station, from which many summer visitors disembarked for the cars and the ride up the Bank. A service tram can be seen at the shelter.

A vista taken from the opposite direction, with Car 1 waiting beyond the loop, with the bridge in the distance. The superb little tram shelter can be seen on the right, with a fine pair of horses representing the alternative modes of transport available.

Car 3 at the same spot in the square. Note that in the early years the trams bore few if any advertisements.

This photograph reveals many interesting details as Car 2, now bearing a board extolling ROCKSIDE HYDRO, pauses at the shelter. Behind the carriage, notices inform that TRAMS START HERE, and that the last car departs at 9 p.m. Note the hoardings by the Crown Hotel, and the individual carrying an advertising board on the right.

Car 1 also carries a ROCKSIDE board as it lingers alongside the superb well cared for three-in-hand horses pulling the charabanc on the left. In the distance a passenger-less Car 3 can be seen on the incline.

A post-First World War scene, with various automobiles posed in shot, and Car 3 loading for the uphill journey. Notice how the camera has flattened out the appearance of the steep one-in-five slope.

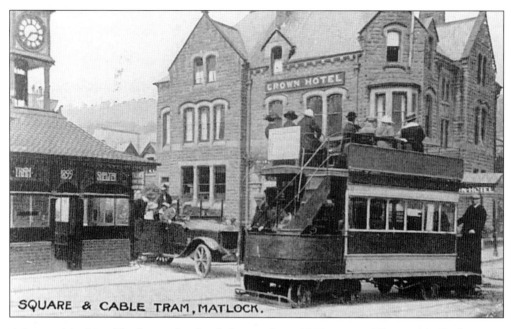

SQUARE & CABLE TRAM, MATLOCK.

A battered-looking Car 1 stops by the shelter in this *c*.1921 picture. There are still almost no adverts on the tram, and a well-loaded motor charabanc is parked alongside the building, replacing the earlier horse-drawn conveyances. Note how the ground actually slopes downwards on the right, before the ascent commences.

Hartley's emporium was one of the major shops in Crown Square, and here a waiting Car 2 poses in front of the well-displayed goods in the double-fronted store windows.

By 1925 the CAR EVERY TEN MINUTES sign had appeared on the shelter. The reason for the demise of the system can be seen on the left, as a Furniss motorbus plies for trade. Though these vehicles were incapable of climbing the steep hill, they touched on both tram termini via a roundabout route.

Two cars pause by Smedley's Hydro in their new livery, after the UDC takeover. They pose in pristine condition, with some elaborate lining-out on the waist panels.

Cars 1 and 2, both sporting ROCKSIDE HYDRO boarding, at rest on the half-way loop at Smedley Street. No. 1 is presumably heading up Rutland Street to the top terminus by the tram depot.

A worse-for-wear Car 2 parks in the same place as the previous shot, with a loaded No. 3 disembarking passengers before heading up to Wellington Street and the bank-top hydros.

Opposite: A good view of the uphill climb as Car 3 prepares for the off, showing good detail of the upper deck of the conveyance. On the down run drivers sometimes slacked off the gripper by the Police Station on the top right, to give lady riders a thrill as the tram careered towards Crown Square apparently out-of-control!

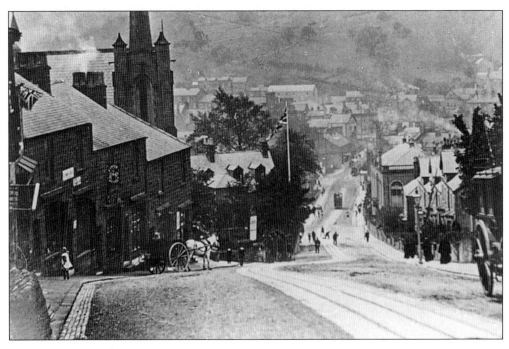

This view, above the Wesleyan Chapel visible on the left, shows not only the steepness of the gradient, but the zigzag bends on the line, all necessitating special pulleys to support the cable in its metal conduit.

Again just above the 110ft steeple of the church, Car 3 pauses on the ascent, with the driver either carrying on a conversation or soliciting trade. The advertising boards on the left feature LUX, ENO'S FRUIT SALTS, and Bakewell Show on 4 August, neatly dating the time of year.

An overloaded Car 1 descends via the sharp curve on Rutland Street on a fine sunny day, with the beauties of Masson Hill opposite well-displayed. Tram travel here on such a day, must have been a distinct pleasure.

A distant cable car approaches the final part of the uphill run, with the tram depot buildings just in shot on the right at the very top of Rutland Street.

A splendid picture of Car 1 and crew at the upper terminus, with dash panels and stairs adorned with advertising. The Corporation logo and gold lining-out show up nicely in this attractive shot, which also picks out another tram on the right, at the level entrance to the shed.

Here a tired-looking Car 1 negotiates floods in Crown Square as it passes the hotel on the left. The tarpaulin visible behind the staircase was presumably to counteract winter draughts.

Two trams pause in a wet and miserable Crown Square, as a policeman joins an inquisitive crowd viewing repairs to the track. There was an underground chamber here, containing a large cable drum which needed greasing fairly regularly. On one occasion the greaser was forgotten, and languished until someone remembered to release him by lifting the manhole cover. His comments were noted, but are unfit for publication!

Summer 1927, and the very end of the cable car service. A dilapidated Car 2 stops in Crown Square, in obvious need of a good clean, and liberally bedecked with advertisements. In this scene, Matlock Bank is on the left.

Car 2 again, with the Crown Hotel behind the tram, and the conductor passing behind the dash panel. Note that the upper deck decency boards now carry adverts.

A final view of the Matlock cable car fleet, with the Car 2 window bill promising a 'BIG NIGHT' with 'YOUNG APRIL'. Note again the hanging tarpaulin, and the decrepit state of the vehicle in its last few months of service.

APPENDIX

CHESTERFIELD TRAMWAYS
Horse Cars   8 November 1882 – 19 December 1904

Fleet No.	Built/Purchased	Builder	Type	Seating
1-2	1882	Ashbury	Open top Eade's type	32
3	1882	Ashbury	Single deck	16
4-5	1890	Milne	Single deck	16
6	1898	Milnes	Single deck	16
7-8	1899	Milnes	Single deck	16
9	1903	Ashbury?	Open top	32

Electric Cars   20 December 1904-23 December 1927

Fleet No.	Year	Builder	Type/Seats	Trucks	Motors/Controllers
1-1	1904	Brush	Open top 22/34	Brush Radial 8ft 6in	Westinghouse 90M 2 x 25hp
13-14	1907	Brush	Open top 22/34	Brush Flexible Axle 8ft 6in	Westinghouse 90M 2 x 25hp
15	1909	Brush	Water Car	Brush Long Base 8ft 6in	Westinghouse 90M 2 x 25hp
16-18	1914	Brush	Balcony 22/34	Peckham P22 8ft	Westinghouse T1 2 x 25hp

Car 17 was destroyed by fire on 20 October 1916 and was rebuilt c.1917. Car 14 was badly damaged in the same fire and was rebuilt as a balcony tram. Between 1918-1919 Cars 6,7,8,11 and 12 were all retrospectively top-covered.

GLOSSOP TRAMWAYS   7 August 1903 – 24 December 1927

Fleet no.	Year	Builder	Type/Seats	Trucks	Motors/Controllers
1-7	1903	Milnes	Open top 22/26	Milnes Girder 6ft	General Electric 58 2 x 35hp
8	1904	BEC	Demi-car 22	BEC 6ft	Brush Raworth
9	1918 (ex-Sheffield)	ERTCW	Single deck	Brill 21E 7ft	General Electric 58 2 x 35hp

MATLOCK CABLE TRAMWAY   28 March 1893 – 30 September 1927

Fleet no.	Year	Builder	Type/Seats	Trucks
1-3	1893	Milnes	Open top 13/18	Bogie
4	1911	Local	Single deck 22	Bogie

No.4 was reconstructed from a double-deck Birmingham cable car, originally built by the Metropolitan Carriage & Wagon Company in 1889. It ceased operations in the autumn of 1914 and was sold off in 1916.

Tramway Managers

Chesterfield (1904-1927)

Robert Lawford Acland	1904-1919
Robert Harry Campion	1919-1924
George Henry Margrave	1925
Walter Gray Marks	1925-1929

Glossop (1903-1927)

Charles Edward Knowles	1903-1927

Matlock (1893-1927)

Job Smith	1893-1898
Thomas Slater	1898
Charles Foster	1898-1915
Ernest Smith	1915-1927